THE DEVELOPMENT OF THEORY AND
PRACTICE IN SOCIAL CASEWORK

THE DEVELOPMENT
OF THEORY AND PRACTICE
IN SOCIAL CASEWORK

By

NINA R. GARTON, M.S.W.

Coos-Curry Mental Health Clinic
Coquille, Oregon

and

HERBERT A. OTTO, Ph.D.

Graduate School of Social Work
University of Utah
Salt Lake City, Utah

With a Foreword by

VIRGINIA SATIR, A.C.S.W.

Mental Research Institute
Palo Alto, California

CHARLES C THOMAS • PUBLISHER
Springfield • Illinois • U.S.A.

Published and Distributed Throughout the World by
CHARLES C THOMAS • PUBLISHER
BANNERSTONE HOUSE
301-327 East Lawrence Avenue, Springfield, Illinois, U.S.A.
NATCHEZ PLANTATION HOUSE
735 North Atlantic Boulevard, Fort Lauderdale, Florida, U.S.A.

*With THOMAS BOOKS careful attention is given to all details of
manufacturing and design. It is the Publisher's desire to present books
that are satisfactory as to their physical qualities and artistic possibilities
and appropriate for their particular use. THOMAS BOOKS will be true
to those laws of quality that assure a good name and good will.*

Printed in the United States of America
D-1

FOREWORD

THIS BOOK IS A careful, scholarly documentation of the ways in which people have viewed and treated human problems for the past hundred years. As such, it gives the modern clinician a real basis for considering the derivation of his present diagnostic and therapeutic practices. And, it encourages him to consider how much of what he is doing really fits today, and how much of it is rooted in a tradition which does not fit the present.

The book demonstrates the existence of a lag between current practices and changing social conditions. It points up that the current understanding of any human condition is very closely tied to therapeutic and diagnostic practices which were formulated in the past. Thus, the book reminds us that some of our practices may well be obsolete.

The study clearly indicates that the same behavior has been viewed and treated differently at different times. Thus, we are reminded how limited we have been, and are, at any given point in time, in our understanding of behavior. By reminding us of this fact I think the book can make us all a little more humble when we set out to label human behavior.

In addition to showing that our ways of analysing behavior do change, this volume also shows that these analyses depend on many things; they depend on how much we know about behavior, what we expect in the way of values and norms, and our generalized pictures of behavior which satisfy the requirements of those norms and values. Since our knowledge is increasing, society's norms and values change from time to time, and the picture of normal behavior also changes. So it behooves those of us who are labelled "change artists" to have real and tangible ways to use the knowledge that is available, and to continue the search for new knowledge. We must also be able to note and use the changes in social values. We must have ways of finding out about expected

v

pictures of behavior if we are to make appropriate diagnoses, and to design commensurate treatment procedures. The presentation of the material focuses on these important issues, and give us a framework in which to consider them.

Clearly, this book should be of value to all people who aspire to understand and change human behavior.

VIRGINIA M. SATIR, A.C.S.W.

INTRODUCTION

IT IS COMMONLY recognized that professions need to pause for reflection; to examine the deeper aspects of their labors and to look beyond daily duties and day-to-day routines. As the broad panorama of the past is examined, new perspectives are opened to the present and future. The social caseworker can gain a deeper understanding of contemporary casework practice and theory by examining such questions as: Is the family the same today as it was in 1882? How did caseworkers meet the changing needs of families from one decade to the next? What were the facts, empirically, in regard to social changes, the family, the caseworker, and casework as they emerged, decade by decade? What are the facts today? What can they presage for the future?

In a broad and general way, 1882 to 1920 was a period of transition from the acceptance of the English Poor Law System to the development of the private charity organization. The recipient of help was literally the poor family. It was the "friendly visitor" of the early nineteen hundreds who preceded the social caseworker of later decades. A milestone in social work history, Mary Richmond's book, *Social Diagnosis,* appeared in 1917 and was recognized as being one of the first compilations of casework knowledge.

The literature refers to the decade of the twenties as the *Age of Economists.* Problems of the time were economic ones. Caseworkers were primarily concerned with such tangible difficulties of their clients as family budgets and the management aspects of homemaking. It was implicit in the casework approach that caseworkers have a knowledge of home economics.

The thirties are significantly known as the Machine Age and were characterized by industrial change and mass replacement of man by machine. The depression, with its nationwide unemployment problems, was a realistic concern of the era. Caseworkers could not meet the clients' financial needs, but they could assist the troubled client by respecting and helping him to respect his individual worth and by giving help in conserving family values. Their efforts, geared to understanding the person, designated the era of the thirties as the *Relationship Period*.

The forties saw the progressive development of "impersonal industry," with all its resulting human problems. Caseworkers borrowed heavily from the field of *psychiatry* in an effort to shed new light on human behavior. Functioning largely in the capacity of *therapists,* many caseworkers looked more toward evaluating the individual client's inner conflicts.

The period of the fifties was characterized by an accelerated trend toward specialization in huge increasingly *automatized industries*. There was an emphasis on conformity with a subsequent devaluation of individuality. Caseworkers found themselves swinging from the individual casework approach of the forties back to an emphasis on the needs of the *entire family*. Group work practice was beginning to make significant gains.

The present era is already being alluded to as the *Age of the Anxious Sixties*. Social change is taking place so rapidly that new dimensions are being added to time and space. Caseworkers are becoming more group-focused as the fate of individuals is recognized to be interrelated with the fate of the group. Our American society is characterized by change—constant, widespread, increasingly rapid change. This phenomena of change can only be understood by gaining a depth perspective of some of the complex social forces which have been at work in the historic development of this nation. Similarly, a thorough knowledge of casework as it is practiced today must be based on an understanding of the development of casework practice and theory from its historic roots to current times.

PREFACE

THIS STUDY came about as the result of an effort to examine how social casework developed, decade by decade, from the late 1800's through the early 1960's in relation to social change and the structure of the family. A need now exists to gain a historical perspective of the inter-relationship of social change and the development of social casework. A study of this type appears to be particularly pertinent at this time due to the growing volume of social welfare legislation placing the profession of social work in the spotlight of public interest.

These are days of constant, rapid, and widespread social change. Social caseworkers, now more than ever before, are involved in assimilating an ever increasing body of knowledge. Professional training emphasizes an awareness of this increasing body of knowledge rather than fixed doctrines. This is reflected in professional training sequences and curriculum changes. There is no escaping the challenges presented by the social changes of the times. Social caseworkers are faced with the problems of how to cope with the conflicts and disparities within our ceaselessly changing social order. This calls for the constant blending of new methods with the old in order to help individuals find solutions to their problems. A major means of incorporating the old and new knowledge is by examining what has transpired in the past.

What were the social changes decade by decade that brought about changes in the family? What were the problems created by social change and the changing family? What were the methods, techniques, and goals of family centered social casework used by caseworkers to meet the ever changing needs of the family?

The focus of this study is primarily on the practice of casework as it evolved. Theory development is traced by examining the ways in which caseworkers were involved in the process of conceptualization and experimental research. In doing this the gap between social casework practice and theory becomes self-evident.

The scope of this study is limited in that only one periodical, *The Family,* was used as it was felt to be the one most representative of the profession of casework. In 1946, *The Family* changed its name to the *Journal of Social Casework,* and in 1950 to *Social Casework.* The first publication of this periodical was in 1920.

Since the first chapter of this volume covers the last part of the 1800's and the early part of the 1900's, prior to the first issue of *The Family,* data was gathered from articles appearing in issues of the *National Conference on Charities and Corrections.* Social changes are many and varied and much in the way of change needed to be left to the reader's imagination.

Articles in the professional journal tended to emphasize the problems and weaknesses of casework due to the profession's continuous search for solutions. The strengths are self-evident in daily practice.

The purpose of this study is to examine the thinking of the writers of the time, specifically caseworkers and those in the profession of social work who shared their practical experiences. This is a cumulative study building on contributions of writers of the times. The hope is that this study will benefit those now practicing in the field of social work and new members entering the field and that it will stimulate intra- and inter-professional dialogue resulting in conscious and planned professional growth.

A study of this kind is not carried on in a vacuum. Many people become involved in the "helping process." One naturally turns to experts for their opinions. The constructive criticism of social worker-sociologists, such as Herbert Bisno, Associate Professor of Sociology at the University of Oregon, Dr. Harold Tascher, Professor of Sociology, University of Montana, and Dr. Gordon Hearn, Director, Graduate School of Social Work, University of Oregon, Portland, Oregon, helped to pinpoint the scope and range of the study, and their observations were of assistance in tightening vague and ambiguous statements. Mrs. Virginia Satir, ACSW Director of Training, Family Project, Mental Research Institute, Palo Alto, California, read the script and gathered impressions from caseworkers already in the field as to clarity and meaning of certain sections of the script.

N. R. G.

H. A. O.

CONTENTS

THE DEVELOPMENT OF THEORY AND
PRACTICE IN SOCIAL CASEWORK

Chapter I

GRASS ROOTS, PERIOD 1882 TO 1920

*It is perhaps the greatest folly of which a nation can be
guilty to attempt to use poverty as a sort of punishment for
offences that it does not send people to prison for. ... We
cannot afford to have poor people anyhow—whether they be
lazy or busy—drinking or sober—virtuous or vicious—thrifty
or careless—wise or foolish. ... It is a public nuisance as
well as a private misfortune. Its toleration is a national crime.*

GEORGE BERNARD SHAW

SOCIAL CHANGE

SOCIAL CHANGE and the family are intimately and inseparably
linked. The social changes that occur reflect changes in the functioning, role, and status of the family. The development of casework services to the family is directly "symbiotically" related to
social change and the resultant changes in the family. This is also
true of development of casework theory.

The Poor Laws of England

*During the period prior to 1920, the English Poor Law System
seemed to have more intensified acceptance in America than in
England.* For this reason it is necessary to examine the English
Poor Law System of the 1800's and early 1900's.

There existed in England in the 1800's a class of employed who
worked in what was referred to as "sweating houses." Pay was
small, hours of work were long and unsanitary working conditions
existed. During this period of sweated work, if a worker fell ill,
the poor law doctor visited and administered to him. If he died,
the Poor Law Authority buried him.

Pay was often so low for day laborers that they received a supplemental sum from public authority charity systems. The sup-

3

plemental sum plus the salary provided minimum sustenance and barely kept a family from starvation.

This system of relief actually appeared to encourage both the growth and continued survival of sweating houses. Trades and employers prospered as a result of this "wage supplement relief system." With only minor changes, this system of relief giving persisted in England until 1821. At that time the English Poor Law Commission examined the relief system. The Commission reached the following significant conclusion which represented a milestone in the practice of English welfare:

> [The existing relief system] . . . will always increase and aggravate the evil it intended to relieve, demoralize the laboring classes, promote idleness and licentiousness among the poor, destroy frugal and industrious habits, impair social affection and throw the burden of maintaining the idle and profligate upon the thrifty and provident.[1]

There appeared to be moral implications that people unable to care for themselves had a moral incapacity for self-help, that their bad times were brought about by misconduct on the part of themselves or other individuals, or a whole community. There was a moralistic evaluation of individuals, such as "drunkard" and "shiftless." The general attitude toward poverty was that the plight of the poor was moral weakness and the way in which it was to be eradicated was by severe administration of relief. Because of the belief that relief encouraged moral failure, some had the opinion that relief should be abolished altogether, thus leaving the destitute to suffer the consequences of their own misconduct. There appeared to be a hard, contemptuous attitude on the part of those who were moderately successful toward those who had failed.

By 1832 the English Poor Law Reform Bill abolished wage supplementation to sweated workers. The assumption appeared to be that any able-bodied person could get a job at which he could make a living and that "if you do not work, you do not eat." Thus,

---

[1] *National Conference of Charities and Correction, 1915.* Chicago, Hildman Printing Co., 1915, p. 438.

the thinking of the times was that the poor must learn to help themselves through work. To be entitled to relief one needed to be destitute, to be a pauper. Thus the Poor Law restricted itself to paupers. Some felt relief should be given only in the almshouse, that the segregation of the poor from society was a way of controlling pauperism. This method meant that entire families were sent to the almshouse, there to be separated from each other and absorbed into institutional life. *In 1909, England passed acts that removed from their statute books forever the accumulation of punitive legislation toward the poor.*

Indoor and Outdoor Relief in America

Many of the attitudes described as being held by the English toward those seeking services and those accepting financial assistance were present in the United States in the 1900's. American indoor and outdoor relief was, in many of its philosophical and organizational aspects, linked to the development of relief giving in England.

PUBLIC INDOOR RELIEF: In this country, prior to 1920, the system of the almshouse, sometimes referred to as the poor house, county farm, or work house, was built and maintained at public expense and controlled by public officials. This type of relief was usually municipal, at a county level, and financed by a county tax. These almshouses often consisted of housing facilities and about one hundred acres of land. All except the bedridden were expected to work. Thus the workers helped to partially pay the expense of maintaining the almshouse. Public Indoor Relief meant that because of lack of income, a whole family, including the children, would be sent to the almshouse. Sending children to almshouses was cheaper than trying to find a home for them The almshouse became a "catchall" for the community's outcasts, a system of segregation of the fit from the unfit, *but there was no segregation of the paupers, the insane, the feebleminded or the aged within the almshouse.*

During the period 1890 to 1899 poor house reform in this country meant the segregation of the various elements within the almshouse, such as the poor, blind, insane, feebleminded, deformed, crippled and epileptics. A movement began to develop which would remove children from the almshouse and place them where they could be given an opportunity to develop normal lives. Eventually, the State assumed the responsibility of supervision and improvement of its municipal institutions. A writer of the times presented a paper at the Conference in 1894 in which he stated:

> The history of the poorhouse has been a disgraceful chapter in the annals of every state and every country. . . . If the vital statistics of poorhouses could be accurately kept, the percentage of deaths from a broken heart would be surprising.[1]

PUBLIC OUTDOOR RELIEF: Prior to 1920, County Commissioners and township trustees doled out what was called "outdoor relief." This relief was controlled by public officials and dispensed by the overseers with no system of records. Outdoor relief was the system for giving relief to those outside the almshouse, that is, those poor persons who remained in their own homes. Overseers, poor masters, or county agents were appointed to give money, or "in kind," such as food, fuel and clothing, where the need existed. At most, public outdoor relief was expected to be only a temporary measure. The relief system for long-time recipients was the almshouse. Many cities and towns used the "work test" to determine the recipient's willingness to work out his own "regeneration." Such labor as "breaking stone" and wood yards were used to provide work for the needy to earn their relief in money or kind. It was widely believed at this time that "giving" to the poor made them paupers and that the average pauper "delights in dirt, disorder, and idleness."[2] *Essentially, outdoor relief was considered to be a danger, because of its tendency to weaken the character and sap the independence of the relief recipients.*

Much consideration was given to determining who were the "honest poor," so as not to confuse them with vagrants and tramps

---

[1] "The Removal of Children From Almshouses," paper presented by Homer Folks, Chairman, Secretary of the State Charities Aid Assoc., of New York. Published by *National Conference of Charities and Correction,* 1894, Isabel C. Barrows (ed), (Boston, George H. Ellis, 1894, p. 119.

[2] Isabel C. Barrows (ed.): *National Conference of Charities and Correction, 1889.* Boston, George H. Ellis, 1889, p. 197.

who were considered to be imposters, hoodlums and beggars, with habits of laziness, shiftlessness, intemperance and vices such as the saloon, the gambling table and the brothel. Vagrants were those with legal residence in a county, while tramps were those who begged from place to place and thus had no legal residence. Tramps were considered to be nomad by their very nature. It was generally believed that if difficulties within a family were caused by such moral conditions as laziness, shiftlessness and intemperance, giving alms was not only detrimental but injurious, and that there was need to "rouse energy and self-control" in these individuals.

The thinking of the time was that monies taken from one class by force, that is by taxation, and given to another class as their right *with no obligation* was NOT charity.[1] There was felt to be a beneficial moral effect upon people if they received charity as a gift which had the attendant connotation of an obligation. Conversely, charity demanded "as a right," was not seen as being beneficial to the receiver. Public outdoor relief, the giving of material relief, soon fell into ill repute. During the period prior to the twenties, some areas abolished municipal outdoor relief altogether. The trend was to private charity as a means of relief giving. The thinking was that those recipients of relief who requested relief from organized private charity as an *obligation* were far less apt to be demoralized by the relief they received. It was widely accepted that recipients of relief needed to feel indebted or obligated for the relief they received.

Private Charity

Gradually administering of indoor and outdoor relief changed to the mobilization of organized private charity to meet the needs of the poor. Charity Organization Societies were formed in 1877 in cities and towns.[2] Their purpose was "private relief giving" and they were supported by voluntary contributions from philanthropic sources. Actually, this was an attempt by commu-

---

[1] *Ibid.*, p. 197.

[2] See page 20 for copy of constitution of a typical Charity Organization Society.

nity-minded individuals to organize relief giving work and to establish some coordination between all private relief giving sources. At the same time, the societies were founded on the idea that the states should leave the field of relief giving assistance to private and religious organizations. The Charity Organization Societies had what they called a four pillar purpose in the helping process: Registration, Investigation, Cooperation, and Friendly Visiting. The organizations were dedicated to a method later referred to as "casework," a function apart from actual relief giving. Some of the organized societies did give relief from their own funds, while others simply made referrals to the proper private charity sources. Problems of the day were the sweating house system, tenement houses, work houses, almshouses, the poor, the beggars, and the giving of alms, sometimes referred to as "handouts."

The private charity organizations at that time were of the opinion that they could and would "provide for every person who should be kept from resorting to public sources of relief."[1] These organizations were founded to counteract what was considered to be the evil influences of indiscriminate and ill-advised "giving." Thus, private charities began to carry the burden of relief giving. Counties discounted relief giving due to what they considered the "unfavorable moral effects," that is, the belief that relief giving increased poverty and suffering and that it even caused the need for the relief that it intended to cure.

As Charity Organization Societies grew, private agencies increasingly were engaged in finding employment for men and women in need of work. As they offered this service, they became concerned over those unable to find employment. Accordingly, this led to the thinking that "social justice" was better than charity. Thus began the search for causes of unemployment and trends to examine the industrial system in relation to poverty. By 1892 some states had passed legislation for free state employment offices in their cities.

---

[1] Edith Abbott: *Some American Pioneers in Social Welfare.* Chicago, University of Chicago Press, 1930, p. 156.

Formation of these private charity organizations was not without criticism. They were taken to task as being too professional, lacking sympathy and giving too little material relief and too much advice. It was also felt that the cost of salaries to get food to the poor was too high, and the private charity organizations were accused of dealing with effects and overlooking the causes of poverty.[1] Interestingly, there was also some recognition that organized private charity might be doing work which the government should be assuming.

THE FAMILY

Social Change and the Family

Prior to the twenties, charity recipients were the poor; those who were destitute. In America, philanthropy, the helping process, had gone through three stages of development: First, the period of institutions such as the almshouse or work for the able-bodied. The second stage was the organization of private Charity Organization Societies with the resultant decline of municipal relief. Thirdly, there was an increased development of a family and community consciousness that marked the emergence of social settlements, including playgrounds, parks and improved housing conditions for families.

The needs of the family at this time were to earn a living wage, have proper housing, sanitary surroundings, recreation and enjoyment. The development of a democratic kind of philanthropy sought to place increasing emphasis on the whole diversified family as a unit of endeavor.

FRIENDLY VISITORS

Personalized Service

The difference between true "charity" and "almsgiving" was being more clearly spelled out during the period of the late 1800's. As friendly visitors began making actual contacts with the needy,

---

[1] *National Conference of Charities and Correction, 1914.* Fort Wayne, Archer Printing Co., 1914, p. 62.

they emphasized "not alms but a friend" and "alms are not too much, but too little." Friendly visiting was regarded as "implying mutual relation deeper and stronger than described by the phrase 'en rapport' and exceeding the best meaning of the phrase 'in touch'."[1] Jane Addams said, " . . . the helper and the helped should be in friendly relations."[2] She did not have a great fear of "pauperizing people" but believed it was the *feeling* with which one received help that determined whether or not the transaction was a pauperizing one; that is, she believed help could be given in such a way as not to increase dependency or make the person feel like a pauper. Relief was not given to those in need without a visit by a friendly visitor, in order to determine whether there was a need for relief; and friendly visitors were making a significant effort to consider need from the point of view of the sufferer.

Churches were assuming considerable responsibility for care of the poor. Later, as the churches became still more active, there seemed to be a change in the then widely prevalent religious belief that poverty was a natural and existent good or evil. The change in the trend of thinking was that poverty and pauperism could in some measure be eradicated. It was considered "scientific charity" at the time to preach to the poor "Thou shalt not beg," and then to the rich, "Thou shalt not give to the able-bodied.[3] Using the appeal that the "actual need of the recipient must first be determined," organized private relief sources solicited the wealthy who were expected to contribute.

Friendly visitors were offering their assistance through devices for help such as sewing rooms for women, wayfarers' lodges where men worked for meals and lodging through preventive and educational work such as sewing and cooking schools. Finally, by offering medical care including advice and encouragement, rather than material aid, they became more concerned with the needs of

---

1 Isabel C. Barrows (ed.): *National Conference of Charities and Correction, 1892.* Boston, George H. Ellis, 1892, p. 458.

2 Isabel C. Barrows (ed.): *National Conference of Charities and Correction, 1897.* Boston, George W. Ellis, 1897, p. 345.

3 Isabel C. Barrows, (ed.): *National Conference of Charities and Correction, 1886.* Boston, George W. Ellis, 1886, p. 176.

the whole family, such as helping a member find employment out of the home, medical care for the sick members and custodial care for those in need of such help.

The development of Settlement houses in neighborhoods was a positive influence in raising the standards of effort of private charity. The neighborhood was now considered as the influence that made it possible, in some way or another, for the underprivileged to become an actual participant in the local social scheme of every day living. The neighborhood settlements were thought to exert a real and permanent democratic influence.

Friendly visitors believed "there was no folly so gross as that which led man to believe that the sorrowing, the baffled, the broken needed no advisors, no encouragers, or inspirers, and that charity that did not evoke a spirit of hope and ambition was considered to be dead charity."[1] Prior to this time, methods such as the work test had been used to sift out the unworthy for rejection, rather than the worthy for assistance. Now efforts were being geared toward cooperation between relief giving sources, but these efforts still had a flavor of preventing duplication rather than effecting coordination. A change from the giving of informal to expert personal service was evident. This change was brought about by a basic shift in viewpoint. It was being increasingly accepted that "cure" of the individual's problem involved the person's character or personality in the vast majority of cases. Conformity to standards of morality was now considered as incidental to the person's problem. It was believed that the moral nature of man raised all his actions above those base desires which led him to intemperance, crime, vice, desertion of family and disregard of duty. This meant that the "poor man" was now seen as being no worse a person than his neighbor.

In 1912, the National Conference devoted an entire section of the conference to Sex Hygiene which indicated more open mindedness, a new frankness and candor in regard to sex problems. At about this same period a new interest emerged in the discovery of

---

[1] *National Conference of Charities and Correction*, 1914. Fort Wayne, Archer Printing Co., 1914, p. 65.

the many other family problems and the question of whether a client or family needed relief became relatively incidental.

During the early 1900's registration (requesting welfare services) and investigation (to determine "worthiness" or eligibility) in casework had strong overtones of a "detective" or "repressive" system designed to eliminate imposters. It was only later in the period that the investigation became a conscientious examination of the needs of individuals and not an inquisition to determine their worthiness.

Mary Richmond pointed out that caseworkers were being referred to as the "middleman," who matched folks and disabilities. She responded that caseworkers had developed a skill of their own in discovering the social relationships by which a given personality or character had been patterned. They had the ability to get at the central core of people's difficulty in relationships and they used their skills to direct action of "mind on mind" which was designed to help individuals understand themselves. She concluded that caseworkers had a skill as well as a point of view of their own and acted as "middleman" only to the extent that a professional caseworker who wanted to do a good all-around job must so act and no further.[1]

Family Centered Casework[2]

The emergence of family centered casework dates back to the turn of the century. At that time, the majority of friendly visitors strongly believed that families as well as individuals needed a friend to foster more self-reliance. Friendly visitors were directing their efforts to educating families and developing within the family activities that would result in more self-help. As an increased awareness of family problems developed, the opinion was expressed that the "family home" was disintegrating, while others felt that the family was merely re-adjusting to the changing out-

---

1 *National Conference of Social Work, 1917.* Chicago, Rogers and Hall, 1917, p. 114.

2 Beginning in 1901 an entire section of the National Conference of Charities and Correction was devoted to "Needy Families in Their Homes," and in 1907 the title of the section was "Needy Families: Their Homes and Neighborhoods," in 1909 "Families and Neighborhoods," in 1914, "Family and Community," and in 1918 "The Family."

side influences. In the past the focus had been more on the "home," than the family, now more focus was being placed on helping family members adjust to changes occurring within the family. Dr. E. Southard is quoted as being "inclined to abolish the family as a unit of interest in social service and replace that unit with the individual,"[1] while others were inclined to feel that members of a family could not be successfully treated without treating the family as a whole. As one member of the Conference stated: "We have not even in our most democratic philanthropy sufficiently emphasized the family, the whole, diversified family . . . as a unit of our endeavors."[2]

Eventually, as the truism developed that nothing could be done for the client but only "with" him, it became evident that the caseworker needed the cooperation of the family at every step if problems were to be worked through which had been recognized by the caseworker but which the family was just beginning to see.[3] Friendly visitors expressed much hesitation about breaking up a home, especially when there were small children and a mother. Even the very poor home was considered better for a child than institutional life. By 1909, the belief had crystallized and had found considerable acceptance that the best care for a child, if possible, was in a home.

The purpose of the investigation in family centered casework during the early 1900's was: (1) to learn the nature of the "disease," as the family was considered to be "socially ailing," and (2) to discover the *strengths* within the family to be used for their recovery toward self-maintenance. There still existed a marked attitude against giving of material relief. However, some change had occurred in the treatment process as more importance was being placed on whether or not material relief should be granted instead of whether recipients were worthy of relief.

In 1917, Mary Richmond prepared a *Manual of Home Service for the Red Cross.* This Manual contained essential principles and

---

[1] *National Conference of Social Work, 1919.* Chicago, Rogers and Hall, 1919, p. 324.

[2] *National Conference of Charities and Correction, 1914,* p. 108.

[3] *National Conference of Social Work, 1918.* Chicago, Rogers and Hall, 1918, p. 286.

methods of social casework and was used in training large numbers of volunteers.[1] During World War I, Red Cross Home Service Chapters were formed all over the country. The primary function of these chapters was to meet the needs of families dependent
upon civilian help, particularly those needs which were beyond
the scope of government help.

During the war period, the importance of the father's role in
the family emerged in very clear perspective. It was recognized
that ways and means of keeping the family closer together needed
to be developed. Efforts were made to consult the absent husband; communication between soldier and family was emphasized; and ways of establishing interests for those left at home
were worked out.

Definitions of Casework

With the turn of the century, attempts were made to define
casework. In 1911, Porter R. Lee defined casework as:

> . . . an attempt to split up a large problem into units and to
> deal with those units efficiently and comprehensively . . .
> whether the units be destitute families, patients, neighbors,
> employees, pupils or sinners.[2]

In 1913, a speaker at the National Conference stated: "Casework
deals with life lived unsuccessfully. Its business is to stir men
and women whose situation is markedly unfavorable, to move on
to a more remunerative plane of effort."[3]

In 1915, Mary Richmond defined social casework as the half of
social work

> . . . which has to do with the social treatment of individuals,
> individual by individual, as distinguished from all those proc-
> esses of social reform which deal with individuals in masses
> . . . the art of doing different things for and with different

---

[1] Mary Richmond: *The Long View*. New York, Russell Sage Foundation 1930, p. 418.

[2] Alexander Johnson (ed.), *National Conference of Charities and Correction, 1911* (Fort
Wayne Printing Co., 1911), p. 260.

[3] *National Conference of Charities and Correction, 1913*, (Fort Wayne: Archer Printing
Co., 1913), p. 353.

people by cooperating with them to achieve at one and the same time their own and society's betterment.[1]

Later, in 1922, in the following decade, Mary Richmond reformulated her definition of social casework.

During 1916, when warnings for preparedness for war were issued to the American Red Cross, all relief-giving agencies turned their attention to war relief in Europe. The trend toward specialization in social work began to develop. Medical social workers and those social workers operating in specialized settings such as hospitals and clinics organized their own specialized groups. It was pointed out that social workers were increasing by the hundreds, but that caseworkers using the method of social work referred to as social casework were increasing more slowly. Casework was now considered a specialty which sought to bring about better adjustment in the social relationships of individual men, women, and children.

Sociology

Since both sociology and social casework dealt with problems of adjustment raised by social contacts and social relations, caseworkers were beginning to incorporate the findings of sociology into their body of knowledge. In a broad sense, they became interested in social problems such as social class, minority problems, migration and mobility, institutions, the community and the person, and the individual and environment. Social casework and its development was now increasingly seen as a scientific technique of making social observations. The findings of sociology thus became an aid in raising philanthropy to a rank of science.

The trend in social work, including social casework, was to consider the causes that led to man's miseries. Some of these causes of social problems were now identified to be tenement houses, intemperance, tuberculosis, and lack of education of the young. Social workers, including caseworkers, ceased to be con-

---

[1] *National Conference of Charities and Corrections, 1915. Chicago,* Hildman Printing Co., 1915, p. 43.

cerned only with the more obvious needs of the poor and under-privileged and began to seek a "wholesome life for all men." In fact, there was so much emphasis on the "social point of view" and identifying the causes of social problems that the development of what was beginning to be called casework (i.e., individual effort) was being neglected. Accordingly in this search for causes, the problems of the poor passed from an affair of the individual to one of the neighborhood, from there to the realm of economics (called "labor and reward"), and finally to the area of health and education. As a result, a spiraling number of progressive and reform movements gathered momentum but are not included within the scope of this study.

Nomenclature

As social changes occurred, a change in the care of the poor took form. Caseworkers found that one of their most difficult problems was a changing vocabulary. The alteration of attitude from "giving of relief" to "treatment and care of needy families" created a need for more versatility in the nomenclature. Words such as "worthy" and "unworthy," "adequate" and inadequate," were no longer being used. The words pauper and pauperism were changed to poverty, dependents, impoverished families, needy families. The phrases "no relief," "work rather than relief" and "unworthy of relief" shifted to such new terms as "adequacy of relief." The words "individual degeneracy" and "hereditary tendencies or inadequacy" were replaced by the words "social uplift." The word "prevention" was being used as in—"preventable causes of poverty."

Charity workers and visitors were now referred to as well-trained friendly visitors and social caseworkers. By 1919, the function of relief giving was seen as being a part of a plan of curative treatment. Increasing recognition was given to the value of the case record, the face-sheet and history as "accumulated experience." As the states assumed supervision of municipal outdoor relief, the pendulum seemed to swing from employment of such phrases as "no relief" to the use of "official relief" and descriptive terms such as "funds for parents," "mother's aid," "widows' pension," "old age pensions," and pensions "for the blind" came into use.

CASEWORK

General Methods

OBJECTIVE APPROACH: For many years Mary Richmond was executive head of a large family agency. In 1911, she joined the Russell Sage Foundation. She had been taking notes on the development and progress of casework for fifteen years. Her book *Social Diagnosis* appeared in 1917 and was an attempt to draw together the basic knowledge of casework up to that time. During this period, a method of social casework was defined and divided into three steps; that is, the gathering of social evidence, the social diagnosis, and social treatment.

Procedures and Techniques

INVESTIGATION AND EVIDENCE: During the early 1900's, obtaining *social evidence* was sometimes still referred to as "the investigation." This meant contacts with the client, the client's immediate family and the gathering of data from outside sources and from documents. Evidence was mainly testimonial in character and was based on actual consultation with the client, plus the outside source of information. In a sense, investigation continued as long as treatment.

Social Diagnosis is defined as:

> . . . the attempt to make as exact a definition as possible of the situation and personality of a human being in some social need —of his situation and personality, that is, in relation to the other human beings upon whom he in any way depends, or who depend upon him, and in relation also to the social institutions of his community.[1]

The social diagnosis was not final, or static, but an attempt to develop as exact a definition as possible of both the social situation and the personality of a given client. The diagnosis was seen

---

[1] Mary Richmond: *Social Diagnosis*. New York, Russell Sage Foundation, 1917, p. 35.

as being fluid since, it could change with later developments in a case and as the social situation of the client was clarified or changed.

Treatment Goals

PLAN OF ACTION: During this period, more emphasis was being placed on gathering social evidence and working out a social diagnosis, while the focus on treatment goals was comparatively neglected. The treatment goal was the plan of action decided upon;[1] the "plan" in most cases being made by the friendly visitor. Treatment goals were spelled out more specifically during the next decade. *However, it is quite clear that during this period family centered social work was the major contributing factor in the origin and development of the casework method for dealing with social problems.*

SUMMARY OF LATE 1800'S AND EARLY 1900'S

Late 1800's

SOCIAL CHANGE: The period of the late 1800's and the early 1900's falls naturally into two decades. The late 1800's saw the beginning of a shift from an agricultural to an industrial economy regulated at the local level. The period reflected influences from abroad such as the laissez faire philosophy that economic problems could be solved by business alone, the influence of the English Poor Law reform system, and Darwinism.

THE FAMILY: Families were laboring under arduous working conditions. A work day was from dawn to dusk. The production of handicrafts or piecework required skill, but the monetary return was not commensurate with the efforts. Child labor was widespread, often under grueling conditions. There was a moral, puritanical attitude toward the dependent including the sick and the poor who were largely the unemployed. There was a prevailing belief that poverty was a permanent and unsolvable condition.

---

[1] *Ibid.*

Pauperism was considered hereditary in character, and it was taken for granted that "people were born that way."

WELFARE WORKERS: The welfare workers of this era were those who provided the welfare services. They were elected officials, political bosses, and other unpaid citizens who assumed responsibility for town government.

Early 1900's

SOCIAL CHANGE: The second era, the early 1900's, saw many social changes, such as the population movement from rural to urban areas, and the continued shifting from an agricultural to an economic industrial economy. There was a sharp distinction between the rich and the poor. The most significant social change was the trend to a more organized program of relief giving. In the early 1900's, approximately 100 cities had American Charity Organization Societies based on individualized services and a friendly attitude to the receiver or client.

THE FAMILY: Social changes brought about changes in the family. The father was leaving the home for employment and continued to work long hours for low pay. Child labor began to diminish and children were leaving the home to attend school.

FRIENDLY VISITORS: Friendly visitors were emphasizing "not alms, but a friend." They began the search for the causes of pauperism, for the needs of the family, for devices of self-help. However, the same influences of the last decade, the efforts to segregate the worthy from the unworthy poor still existed. Training for friendly visitors placed emphasis on home economics and homemaking.

CASEWORK: The trends in the practice of casework during this period saw the beginning of a change in attitude toward the poor, with a resultant change in the meaning of relief. Methods were now more inclusive, as efforts were made to assess the social situation, the personality, and social need of the receiver. Treatment in casework still consisted mainly of the plan of action decided upon by the helper, a "managing" approach.

THE CHARITY ORGANIZATION SOCIETY OF[1]

CONSTITUTION

Article I

The name of this society shall be "The Charity Organization Society of
--."

Article II

This society shall be conducted upon the following principles:—
1. Every department of its work shall be completely severed from all question of religious belief, politics and nationality.
2. The society shall not directly dispense alms in any form.

Article III

The objects of this society are:—
1. To prevent children from growing up as paupers.
2. To encourage thrift, self-dependence and industry, through friendly intercourse, advice and sympathy and to help the poor to help themselves.
3. To raise the needy above the need of relief, prevent begging and imposition and diminish pauperism.

To accomplish these objects, it is designed:—
1. To provide that the case of every applicant for relief shall be thoroughly investigated and the results of such investigation placed at the disposal of the public officer having charge of the poor, of all the churches and charitable societies of _____ and of private persons of benevolence.
2. To obtain employment, if possible; if not, to obtain, so far as necessary, suitable assistance for every deserving applicant from benevolent individuals, churches, etc.
3. To make all relief, whether by alms or charitable work, conditional upon good conduct and progress.

Article IV

The society shall be composed of the following persons:—
1. Members of District Commitees.
2. Annual members (any person who shall subscribe not less than $2.00 to the society annually).

----

[1] Isabel C. Barrows (ed.): *National Conference of Charities and Correction,* 1887. Boston, George H. Ellis, 1887, pp. 140-141.

3. Life members (any person who shall subscribe $25.00).

4. Ex-officio members, the public officer having charge of the poor, and one delgate from each of the churches and charitable society of _____.

Article V

The management of the society shall be vested in a Central Council, which shall have the control of all questions of principle and all matters relating to the work of the society;—

The Central Council shall consist of:—

1. Two delegates from each District Committee of the society.

2. The ex-officio members of the society.

The officers of the council shall consist of a president, vice-president, secretary, treasurer, and one or more agents and shall be elected by ballot at the first meeting of the council after the annual meeting of the society.

The officers of the council shall be the officers of the society.

There shall be a regular meeting of the council on the last Friday of each month and special meetings may be called by an officer with the concurrence of three members.

At any meeting of the council, five members, other than ex-officio members shall constitute a quorum.

Article VI

The town (or village) shall be divided, for the purposes of the society, into such districts as the council may designate; and the council may at any time rearrange such districts.

In each district there shall be a committee of three or more residents. The council shall appoint the members of such committee. Each District Committee shall, subject to the control of the council, manage the work of the society within its district; and each District Committee shall deal only with the cases of persons resident in its district.

It shall be the duty of a committee of a district to see that every application from persons living within the district is thoroughly investigated; to study how applicants for relief can be raised into independence and to make them self-supporting, whenever possible; to obtain aid for deserving applicants, unable to earn their support from the appropriate sources; to see that all children in the district attend school; to try to secure a good sanitary condition of the district; to see that such reports are made to the Central Council as the latter shall require.

Article VII

An annual meeting of the society shall be held at such time and place, in or about the month of _____, as the council may designate; and the council may call special meetings of the society.

Article VIII

This Constitution shall not be amended except by the resolution of a two-thirds vote of a meeting of the council, at which at least ten members, other than ex-officio members, shall be present, due notice of such amendment having already been given at a previous stated meeting of the council.

REFERENCES

Books

Abbott, Edith: *Some American Pioneers in Social Welfare.* Chicago, University of Chicago Press, 1930.

Richmond, Mary: *Social Diagnosis.* New York, Russell Sage Foundation, 1917.

_____: *The Long View.* New York, Russell Sage Foundation, 1930.

Proceedings

Wright, A. O. (ed.): *National Conference of Charities and Correction,* 1883. Madison, George H. Ellis, 1885.

National Conference of Charities and Correction, 1886. Boston, Geo. H. Ellis, 1886.

National Conference of Charities and Correction, 1887. Boston, Geo. H. Ellis, 1887.

National Conference of Charities and Correction, 1888. Boston, Geo. H. Ellis, 1888.

National Conference of Charities and Correction, 1889. Boston, Geo. H. Ellis, 1889.

National Conference of Charities and Correction, 1890. Boston, Geo. H. Ellis, 1890.

National Conference of Charities and Correction, 1891. Boston, Geo. H. Ellis, 1891.

National Conferenec of Charities and Correction, 1892. Boston, Geo. H. Ellis, 1892.

National Conference of Charities and Correction, 1893. Boston, Geo. H. Ellis, 1893.

National Conference of Charities and Correction, 1894. Boston, Geo. H. Ellis, 1894.

National Conference of Charities and Correction, 1896. Boston, Geo. H. Ellis, 1896.

National Conference of Charities and Correction, 1897. Boston, Geo. H. Ellis, 1897.

National Conference of Charities and Correction, 1899. Boston, Geo. H. Ellis, 1899.

National Conference of Charities and Correction, 1900. Boston, Geo. H. Ellis, 1900.

National Conference of Charities and Correction, 1902. Boston, Geo. H. Ellis, 1902.

National Conference of Charities and Correction, 1903. Fred J. Heer, 1903.

National Conference of Charities and Correction, 1904. Fred J. Heer, 1904.

Johnson, Alexander (ed.): *National Conference of Charities and Correction,* 1905. Fred J. Heer, 1905.

National Conference of Charities and Correction, 1906. Fred J. Heer, 1906.

National Conference of Charities and Correction, 1907. Indianapolis, Wm. B. Burford, 1907.

National Conference of Charities and Correction, 1908. Fort Wayne, Fort Wayne Printing Co., 1908.

National Conference of Charities and Correction, 1909. Fort Wayne, Fort Wayne Printing Co., 1909.

National Conference of Charities and Correction, 1910. Fort Wayne, Archer Printing Co., 1910.

National Conference of Charities and Correction, 1911. Fort Wayne, Archer Printing Co., 1911.

National Conference of Charities and Correction, 1912. Fort Wayne, Archer Printing Co., 1912.

(From 1913 on there was no *editor* of Conference volumes.)

National Conference of Charities and Correction, 1913. Fort Wayne, Archer Printing Co., 1913.

National Conference of Charities and Correction, 1914. Fort Wayne, Archer Printing Co., 1914.

National Conference of Charities and Correction, 1915. Chicago, Hildman Printing Co., 1915.

National Conference of Charities and Correction, 1916. Chicago, Hildman Printing Co., 1916.

National Conference of Social Work, 1917. Chicago, Rogers and Hall, 1917.

National Conference of Social Work, 1918. Chicago, Rogers and Hall, 1918.

National Conference of Social Work, 1919. Chicago, Rogers and Hall, 1919.

Chapter II

POST WORLD WAR I, DECADE 1920-1929

*The strength of a nation does not lie, like that of an army,
in the uniformity of its members, but in the variety and
strength of the different characters which can be brought to
work harmoniously within it; and it is in the Family that
this variety and strength of character is nourished.*

HELEN BOSANQUET

SOCIAL CHANGE

Change and Transition in Urban Living

IN THE URBAN AREAS, small businesses such as the corner store were giving way to organized systems of chain stores. This social change contributed to the creation of labor conflicts. Standardizing of factory products became a reality. This period was the beginning of an era of prosperous times, with trends to installment buying. There was a transition of the house family to living quarters in small apartments or hotels. The trend toward increased interests outside the home caused a decline in neighborliness and neighborhood ties. These were tangible changes, and they brought about many subtle changes more difficult to recognize. In the rural areas, farmers too were having their problems.

THE FAMILY

Social Change and the Family

The family was considered to be an institution with eight functions, namely: economic, status giving, educational, religious, recreational, protective, affectional, and reproductive.

A significant hallmark of social transition was the emancipation of women. Women were entering the fields of economics, social and civic life. This trend toward equality seemed to create a lessening of respect for authority within the family. Divorce became more acceptable as a solution to marital problems. Another sign of change was the more outspoken interest in sex. Parents began thinking in terms of controlling the number of children in the family either by choice or by planning. *The emancipation of women brought about a change in the roles of family members and marked the passing of male dominance within the family.*

THE CASEWORKER

Development of Formal Training

As indicated in the previous chapter, during the years 1914-1918, social caseworkers turned to the problems created by the emergency of World War I. Following the war, they again turned to casework. Voluntary private agencies were now carrying the responsibility of casework services to clients.

At the onset of this era, the best qualified caseworkers were considered to be those who had training in home economics. The emphasis was economic, that is, the giving of relief. Mothers were given help in becoming better homemakers. Helen Hanchette wrote:

> Home economics is to the home what girders are to the large building. A well-organized system of income and outgo, coupled with skill in management, will cause a household to run without apparent effort.[1]

Later in this period, as the caseworker became involved in successes or failures in cases, there was an increased trend toward examining the emotional equipment of the caseworker, her educational training and work experience. The thinking of the time was that since at every turn in the progress of a case the caseworker's personality was involved, her first responsibility was to study her own reactions and maintain a detachment that would keep her emotionally free.[2] Caseworkers were seen as having been born

---

[1] Helen W. Hanchette: Home economics as a working force in family casework, *The Family*, II (July, 1921), p. 111.

[2] Elizabeth H. Dexter: The social case worker's attitude and problems as they affect her work. *The Family*, VII (October, 1926), p. 195.

with certain personality qualities coupled with an education which supplemented and complemented these qualities.

The research involved in analyzing case records provoked anxiety in caseworkers. Case records were being discussed and analyzed in terms of results, that is, in terms of success of cases, of failure, and in accounting for the action taken. Biased attitudes of caseworkers toward social classes, sex, religion, and certain races were identified and recognized as interfering with the practice of casework. Emphasis was increasingly placed on a higher quality of maturity and increased education for caseworkers. Particular recognition was given to the special need for educational courses on the family and for more knowledge of cultural differences. On the subject of cultural differences, volunteer private agencies lamented: "Our workers are so helpless to deal with these problems of immigrants that they tend to neglect them altogether."[1]

Family Centered Casework

The changes in giving of "relief" brought about a new emphasis on family centered casework. One author stated: "This is the gamut through which social casework has developed, 'charity' denoted an attitude, the family denotes a social institution."[2] Thus, focus of the helping process moved from that of "charity" to the "family approach," emphasizing the family as a unit.

> One of the most important of all conditions for success in family life is continuity of its membership. It was discovered that it is better to spend time and money in trying to make a present home fit for the child, than to transfer it to another, even though a much better one. In a literal sense the family is the conservation and transmitter of the social gains of the ages; without it we should fall back into a state even lower than that of savages.[3]

---

[1] Mary E. Hurlbutt: Invisible environment of an immigrant, *The Family*, IV, October, 1923, p. 160.

[2] Frank J. Bruno: The meaning of the conference, *The Family*, VIII, December, 1927, p. 262.

[3] *Ibid.*, p. 266.

Actual practice in regard to the welfare of children lagged behind theory, for children continued to be removed from the home.

Recording and Fact Finding

The continued trend to family centered casework stimulated efforts to discover how change in clients was brought about through casework. As early as 1921, Virginia Robinson stated that it would be necessary for caseworkers to record what had transpired.

> In the records [of family casework] I have found so few illustrations [of how change of attitude was accomplished] that one must conclude that these recordings have slipped in by accident and that it is not the practice or the intention . . . *to record* any of the processes by which the work of reeducation is brought about unless some manipulation of the environment is made.[1]

Caseworkers were recording their work, but for a period of two years no significant findings were revealed from their records. They were concerned about their procedures; (what steps to take in regard to the clients' requests for help with their problems), but their primary concern was their inability to explain *why* they did what they did. It was soon recognized that any analysis of the processes of casework would have to be carried on by the caseworkers themselves. *Thus, the whole movement of "evaluation," and what was being accomplished in casework had its beginnings in the medium of the case record.*

Individual interviews were analyzed for skill, techniques, and procedures. The problem of separating "treatment" from "information-getting" in the case record was not believed to be possible. The study of case records revealed that casework concerned with the client's internal problems meant the caseworker was more involved in "thinking" than "doing." It meant caseworkers needed to analyze and interpret their cases while recording them. From these findings, chronological as opposed to topical record-

---

1 Virginia Robinson: Analysis of processes in the records of family caseworking agencies. *The Family,* II, July, 1921, p. 103.

ing developed. Topical recordings were the result of "the investigation" and the accumulated data was recorded by topics such as family composition, economic condition, and medical history. Thus, chronological recordings evolved as a result of a decrease in "investigations" by caseworkers and more toward recordings as they developed interview by interview. An example of chronological recording:

> Mrs. F. returned shortly after with some groceries. I had no difficulty in establishing a friendly contact because Mrs. F. was aware that she was to have a new worker and was anxiously awaiting my visit. She gave me a chair between the kitchen and Mr. F.'s bedroom so that he could join in the conversation. Mrs. F. immediately launched upon the subject which was most important to her . . .[1]

By 1926 caseworkers were making some progress in analyzing treatment methods in casework. There was a need to develop a way to measure the growth of the "personality" in order to measure success of treatment of clients' internal problems. Lengthy guides were outlined for caseworkers so that they could attempt to measure success and failure in casework. Recording of cases became more subjective, incorporating what the caseworker did and the "why" of her own mental processes and conscious behavior.

A further effort was made to check thousands of family casework records.[2] The results of this fact finding was the development of a working hypothesis that would be conducive to future research. It was anticipated that results of this work would also eventually lead to the development of a program of education for caseworkers.

Caseworkers felt that clients were often unresponsive and that one of the most urgent problems was the worker's lack of understanding about the human personality. Dorothy Kahn stated, "It is the failures that keep finding us out . . . We have a constitutional incapacity for admitting failure." Sooner or later, she com-

---

[1] Helen P. Kempton: The class teaches itself, *The Family*, X, April, 1929, p. 50.

[2] Bruno: *op. cit.*, p. 261.

mented, caseworkers would be forced to exercise more selection in accepting clients for services as there was a relationship of this factor of selection in the achievement of success in casework.[1]

Caseworkers during the period of the twenties felt they had the problem of "being pressed for time." They believed they were overworked, and that there was a lack of public understanding of what they were attempting to do. There was a steady increase in volume of work as more emphasis was placed on casework services when relief was requested. Attitudes of the general public were slowly changing from intolerance to more understanding and tolerance of poverty, and caseworkers were placing more emphasis on keeping the family together.

Research

The two years, 1922 to 1924, were years of extensive "soul searching" for caseworkers involved in the practice of social casework. They were years of analysis of casework and development of research. The long search for a way of measuring activity in case records was materializing and contrary to the belief of many, a possibility now seemed to exist of developing objective criteria for measuring the effectiveness of casework. Based on the findings of the studies conducted, Harold A. Phelps concluded:

> The urgent need of the present in organizing the case record for research and treatment of any social problem, points decidedly to the acceptance of a standardized procedure in the collection of facts. Though arduous and often of no immediate significance, it is the beginning of sound diagnosis and the only method by which the *results* of treatment may be evaluated.[2]

Thus began two approaches to a scientific method in casework, the *statistical method* and the *case study*. What was found in analysis of the collected data was not encouraging.

---

[1] Dorothy C. Kahn: The need for interpretation of trends and accomplishments in family social work, *The Family*, VIII, July, 1927, p. 152.

[2] Harold A. Phelps: The case record and scientific method, *The Family*, VIII, June, 1927, p. 108.

Statistical Method: This method had a working hypothesis designed to protect the worker from the "blind gathering of facts." There were clearly defined units or norms, or a working vocabulary, for collecting statistics, such as single, married, divorced, widow, deserted, American-born, foreign-born. Next in the procedure was the gathering and storing of the facts thus obtained. By this method, statistics were secured regarding marriage, widowhood, divorce, desertion, old age, illegitimacy, juvenile delinquency. The accumulation and analysis of these statistics indicated tendencies and trends such as:

SOCIO-ECONOMIC STATUS OF TWENTY-THREE FAMILIES

	Number
Receiving relief	20
Both parents living	21
Father in poor health	15
Mother in poor health	7
One parent alcoholic	12
Father unemployed	11
Mother employed	6
Father deserted	5
Mother "unfaithful" to husband	3
Father psychotic	2
Father in prison	1[1]

Case Study Method

This was another scientific approach designed to measure casework. Researchers working with case records were asking for more recording and these "grew like yeast." In the search for casework methodology, case records were being studied like textbooks. However, case records were criticized as being "dry as dust" to read. As a result, caseworkers attempted to better organize their recordings, adapting the record to the problem or problems, and to separate objective and subjective material while maintaining a comprehensive approach to the over-all problem.[2] As a result of

---

[1] Phyllis Blanchard and Richard H. Paynter: Socio-psychological status of children from marginal families, *The Family*, VIII, March, 1927, p. 4.

[2] See the illustration of how caseworkers were attempting to analyze their own mental processes, p. 44-51.

the findings in the case record, articles began to appear in professional journals concerned with the character, frequency, incidence, association, and adjustability of certain case problems. Syndromes were being identified whereby groupings could be made for further study. Different problems, it was found, had different rates of adjustment. Of particular significance was the detection of chronic cases that seemed more or less hopeless from the standpoint of effecting adjustment. Another result of continued research indicated caseworkers were using "persuasion," were giving "advice." *One outstanding discovery was that the cases studied showed a lower percentage of success than had been anticipated.*[1]

By 1929, both the *statistical* and the *case study* method of research were well established. The momentous discovery in research as this time was "dependency." The major question of the times became: Is casework tending toward perpetuation of pauperism and dependency? That is, "Was casework geared to developing resourcefulness of families so they would be capable of eventually helping themselves instead of relying on the caseworker?"[2]

Another important development flowing from the use of research methods was the recognition by caseworkers that time was slowly but surely changing family roles.

Psychology

During the twenties, psychological testing of character and emotions was being developed, but these tests were looked upon as offering only "dead parts," and were considered to be of little use in casework. There was some exploration of how mental tests could be used in casework. In the early part of this period, the thinking was that, although psychological tests might be of some value, the best way to evaluate an adult's capacities was to obtain knowledge of the individual through observation in his home, at

---

[1] Phelps: *loc. cit.*

[2] Ellen F. Wilcox: The measurement of achievement in family casework, *The Family,* VIII (April, 1927), p. 46.

work, and in his social activties. There was general agreement that caseworkers could then make evaluations from the standpoint of the client's truthfulness, affection, sympathy, cleanliness, promptness, responsibility, and stability."[1] Psychiatric and psychological approaches were looked upon as interesting and scientific but were considered "abstract and remote" from the living individual particularly when compared with the attempts of the caseworker to understand personality as a living process.

Psychiatry

Jessie Taft stated: "Psychoanalytic literature is too technical and too far in advance of most of our thinking to be convincing."[2] Later, with the development of social psychiatry she noted:

> "It was inevitable, with the interest in psychological interpretations which animated the group of psychiatrists, Dr. Adolf Meyer, Dr. August Hoch, Dr. Thomas Salmon, that their peculiar contributions to *social* psychiatry should have been on the side of a dynamic interpretation of behavior."[3]

By 1926, developments in psychiatry focused on the mentally ill, mental hospitals, mental hygiene clinics for the mentally ill, and then finally reached out to the preventive approach. It was during the latter part of this era, 1926 to 1929, that psychiatry definitely began to be incorporated into the framework of casework practice.

Social Psychiatry

This was a method of approach to human beings not specifically confined to the development of a specialized form of social treatment for mental patients but applicable to all persons. Signifi-

---

1 William Healy: The application of mental tests in family casework, *The Family,* II, July, 1921, p. 100.

2 Jessie Taft: The effect of an unsatisfactory mother-daughter relationship upon the development of a personality, *The Family,* VII, March, 1926, p. 14.

3 Jessie Taft: The relation of psychiatry to social work. *The Family,* VII, November, 1926, p. 200.

cantly, the focus of this approach was in *relating* rather than in separating normal and abnormal behavior. Mental health was conceived as the concern of every human being. This was the beginning of the "coming together" of psychiatry and social casework.[1] Social psychiatry soon became the chief tool of the social caseworker. A hypothesis on which to base a diagnosis now included a treatment plan for the personality and behavior difficulties of the client. This marked the first acceptance of the fact that the early experiences of a child profoundly influenced his behavior later in life. Actually, this meant that every kind of behavior was seen as an attempt to adjust. This understanding marked the emergence and use of knowledge of human growth and behavior in casework. In 1928, Jessie Taft stated that it was an illuminating discovery that an individual was never just "born that way," and that . . .

> Like everything else in a world of cause and effect, a man could be explained in terms of his particular history; his personality, his behavior could be accounted for in large measure because he had acquired them in the course of his lifetime. Then there was added the corollary that not only was his behavior acquired, instead of being imposed by a fixed heredity, that it is always an effort at adjustment. It serves a purpose to the individual however bizarre or apparently unprofitable it may seem.[2]

Through this contribution from psychiatry, the "psychology of casework" was transformed, terminology was changed, and the focus was shifted.

Casework Definitions

More specific and inclusive definitions of casework were evolving. Mary Richmond, in her book *Social Diagnosis*, stated the trained social worker needed the ability to combine: (1) her insight into understanding of the individuality and personal characteristics of clients; (2) her insight into use of resources and en-

---

[1] *Ibid.*, p. 201.

[2] Jessie Taft: The spirit of social work, *The Family*, IX, June, 1928, p. 105.

vironment; (3) her use of direct action of mind-on-mind, and (4) use of indirect action through the social environment in such a manner as to better enable the individual to make those adjustments that develop his personality.[1]

In *What is Social Casework*, Mary Richmond offered a more precise definition of casework: "Social casework consists of those processes which develop personality through adjustments consciously effected, individual-by-individual, between men and their social environment."[2] In the conclusion of her book, she stated the highest test of social casework was growth in personality of the client, and that the caseworker, therefore, needed to answer the following questions: Does the personality of the client change and change in the right direction? Are energy and initiative released in the direction of "higher and better wants and saner social relations?" She pointed out that only an instinctive reverence for the personality of the individual and a warm human interest in people, as people, could win for the social caseworker an affirmative answer to these questions. An affirmative answer meant growth in personality for the caseworker too; the service was reciprocal. The difference in approach of the psychiatrist was defined as: "Beginning near the center of a problem of diseased personality, the psychiatrist bores in and in, while the social worker's sphere of action radiates outward along all the lines of a client's social relations."[3]

Jessie Taft, a contemporary of Mary Richmond, also placed the major emphasis on the psychological changes of the client. More specifically, she stated:

> The social worker, thus far, has specialized in the manipulation of environmental factors and social resources. She is now realizing that casework is always fundamentally psychological . . . and that environment is never external to the psychology of the client.[4]

---

1 Book Review, *The Family*, III, Mary, 1922, p. 70.

2 Mary Richmond: *What is Social Casework?* New York, Russell Sage Foundation, 1922, p. 70.

3 *Ibid.*

4 Jessie Taft: The problem of casework with children, *The Family*, I, July, 1920, p. 2.

A year prior to Mary Richmond's definition of social casework, Virginia Robinson had evaluated casework as: (1) Observation and assembling of facts; (2) hypothetical interpretation of these facts, and (3) control of facts for new ends.[1]

One writer of the times, Mary S. Brisley, was less optimistic in regard to defining casework stating there were no words for the action of "man upon man," or how a change of attitude in the client was accomplished. In analyzing case records, she stated there was . . .

> . . . danger of rationalization, the lack of a professional vocabulary, the constant need of qualifying statements and the apparent impossibility of putting into words the essential quality—process—call it what you will, which accomplished the result.[2]

One of the most specific definitions of casework was given by Frank Bruno when in 1925 he wrote:

> Social casework must assume as its major responsibility the task of determining whether men are successfully meeting the demands of the functions they are called upon as social beings to perform, and to aid them to a more successful participation when they have failed.[3]

To some writers the essence of casework was an **artistic skill**.

> Caseworkers are attempting to define their methods of approach to clients, their ways and means of getting results, thus representing to all intents and purposes a step in the transition of casework from a philosophy to a scientific process. Our ultimate goal, however, is a step beyond this, for, as Miss Richmond has pointed out, casework at its best should be not a scientific, but an artistic skill.[4]

---

[1] Robinson: *op. cit.*, p. 101.

[2] Mary S. Brisley: An attempt to articulate processes. *The Family*, V, October, 1924, p. 157.

[3] Frank Bruno: Family social work, *The Family*, VI, July, 1925, p. 142.

[4] Helen P. Kempton: Skill in casework, *The Family*, IX, December, 1928, p. 260.

Professional Vocabulary

The lack of a professional vocabulary was very apparent to the social worker of the twenties. Problems in semantics and nomenclature were evident. Continued efforts were being made to obtain some kind of uniform agreement on the definitions of the terms that were in use all over the country. This was the result of caseworkers attempting to define more precisely their procedures and analyze their actions. Determined attempts were being made at this time to articulate processes in casework and to clarify methods. Some of the processes were considered to be "getting to know the client," establishing a sympathetic atmosphere, maintaining a professional attitude, building up the client's self respect, planning with the client. As one writer explained:

> Two years ago I doubt whether I would have used the word "techniques" so generously, in connection with social casework. At that time I was having "processes" firmly rooted in my vocabulary . . . it did not occur to me that "processes" could be further analyzed.[1]

The process in casework was now seen as being comprised of many techniques. A two year study of techniques of interviewing revealed eighty-six different techniques. Some of these were "explaining the agency," "appeal to reason," and "flattery." An avid interest in the articulation of processes of casework was evident. There were those who felt there would always be some elements in casework that would be fluid and unanalyzable. Also, some changes in casework through the passage of time were considered inevitable. It was anticipated that meanings of words would change and that there would be new additions to the vocabulary.

CASEWORK

General Methods

OBJECTIVE CASEWORK APPROACH: Caseworkers were being realistic in their general approach to the fast-moving world of 1920. The caseworker was expected to obtain exhaustive data about the

---

[1] Pearl Salsberry: Techniques in casework, *The Family*, VIII, July, 1927, p. 153.

client from as many sources as possible. The emphasis of casework was not to know the person *but to know all about him.* However, relatives of clients were looked upon more as financial resources than as reliable sources of information.[1] It was felt that in the past caseworkers had been so concerned with economic factors and the giving of relief that this factor alone had actually obsessed their thinking . . . "resulting in failure in casework and no real progress in family rebuilding in far too many cases."[2] Casework methods of the time were more objective and corrective and emphasized dealing with particular situations.

By 1923, caseworkers were beginning to feel that the expenditure of financial assistance could be used as an opportunity for client education. They found that clients who needed financial assistance had other problems that were affecting family life. *The change taking place was a shift from the giving of material assistance to treating the person, or to a combination of both financial help and casework services.*

SUBJECTIVE CASEWORK APPROACH: As caseworkers became more concerned with the client's internal problems, there was an attempt to develop greater skill in what was then called "influencing the conscious inter-relation between mind and mind," as an aid in the development of the "personality" of the client. To accomplish this, the caseworker needed to use her own personality. It was the effect of the caseworker's personality, attitude, and manner on the client that was seen as bringing about change in the client. How this change in the client was brought about was not, as yet, known. As a result, there was a general recognition that caseworkers needed to be more analytical in their evaluation of both the social and the psychological causations of their client's problems.

By 1926, caseworkers stated that by helping clients change their point of view and habits of thought they helped them to see themselves in relation to their situation and thus become more effective human beings. Both inner and outer influences were

---

[1] The cooperation of relatives, *The Family,* II, November, 1921, p. 163.

[2] Bruno: *Family Social Work,* p. 145.

seen as bringing about a change in the client's point of view.[1] The search continued to secure more knowledge on how change in individuals was brought about and for more concrete methods to be used in casework treatment.

It was found that often the client's stated problem was not the source of the difficulties. As case records became more complete, the client's original request when the case was opened and what the caseworker actually did were being explored. As studies of case records continued, a casework process was developing; and a general method began to emerge.

Procedure and Techniques

THE INVESTIGATION: In 1920, the specific plan or the procedure for casework was called "the investigation" meaning "verification of the applicant's story." The social diagnosis was made from the available data. There was a continued "looking to the future" in the hope that psychiatry and psychology would offer more under-standing of the client. The caseworker was being encouraged to use resourcefulness and imagination in helping clients solve their problems, but getting the facts appeared to be an obsession.

> So many false starts in casework arise because we do not know the facts. The facts often involve the clients making dif-ficult admissions—crimes committed, untruths told, poor fam-ily background, failures to conform to social conventions, and the many secrets which human beings conceal through shame or fear. The trend in thinking was that any techniques which would help to make these admissions easier would tend to place casework on a foundation of rock . . .[2]

In 1927, Jessie Taft referred to the use of "transference" in case-work, stating it was being used consciously by psychoanalysts and unconsciously by the caseworker to "vitalize plans and ideas."[3]

---

[1] Jessie Taft: *The Spirit of Social Work*, p. 105.

[2] Salsberry: *op. cit.*, p. 157.

[3] Jessie Taft: The use of the transfer within the limits of the office interview, *The Family*, V, October, 1924, p. 140.

Caseworkers were vague in defining the use they were making of the transference.

Casework techniques continued to be mainly "environmental manipulation," for example, removing a behavior problem from the home to a private school, helping a client change to more suitable employment, help in making a move to another neighborhood, or leaving the city to live on a farm.

SOCIAL SERVICE EXCHANGE: In 1923, the Social Service Exchange was born and was used as a technique in the investigation. Apparently, the Exchange was originally conceived as a "fraud-prevention force," but this was soon discarded and the Exchange was used primarily to avoid duplication of services between agencies. The Exchange consisted of a card index of families and individuals in whom various social, medical, or religious agencies of the community were, or had been, interested. Cards bore only identifying information, that is: names, ages, and addresses and the names of agencies who had known the family. Use of the Exchange eventually and inevitably resulted in a sharing of experiences and a working together of those agencies giving service to the client.[1]

THE INTERVIEW: The purpose of the interview was to help the client free himself from conflicts.[2] Clients were given more time for reactions to material discussed in the interview, for it was believed that

> . . . to stimulate a client into formulating plans immediately following an unburdening, has proven to be futile sufficiently often to warn against it. On the other hand, giving the client time to settle down to the comfortable feeling of being free to think and to make his decisions has over and over again brought the best results.[3]

The trend in interviewing techniques was directed to the assumption that if the client was given an opportunity to associate

---

[1] Arthur Dunham: The elements of a successful social service exchange, *The Family,* III, February, 1923, p. 246.

[2] Anna Vlachos: Opening the way, *The Family,* V, October, 1924, p. 153.

[3] *Ibid.,* p. 154.

freely, widely, and deeply around the problems he was facing in his daily living, he would reveal himself to himself. This revelation would then provide the motivation for the client to make constructive changes in himself and in ways of dealing with his problem. The caseworker participated by assisting the client in clarifying his thinking, by making suggestions, and by leaving the client free to make his own decision. This new procedure brought about a lessening in zeal for prompt and adequate investigation. Now the concern was what to do with the information after it had been obtained.

A study was made of nine interviews to analyze and determine the specific techniques used in the successful casework interview. The techniques that constantly recurred were: "Build up a basis of cooperation before presenting an important plan; maintain a professional attitude and guard against emotion on your part; plan with the client; put the initiative up to the client whenever possible."[1] *By 1924, the interview was recognized as the principal technique in casework.*

Differences in techniques of caseworkers were now being more clearly defined. A number of caseworkers began to stress the importance of the emotional "relationship" between client and worker. This was defined as an emotional "going over" of the client to the caseworker. As one writer explained, this "mutual understanding" would break down old fears and inhibitions in clients and would provide a safe medium in which the growth of new thoughts, feelings, and habits would become possible.[2] Other caseworkers felt successful readjustments of families and individuals came from practical use of resources and education of clients through ideas and rational appeals.

By 1928, Mary Richmond's "mind-on-mind" technique was being called "worker-client relationship." Proponents of the viewpoint that casework was an art stressed the use of originality.

Continued examination of case records indicated that certain clients receiving casework services over the years had shown no improvement. Casework with "drinkers," as they were referred to

---

1 Brisley: *op. cit.,* p. 157.

2 Taft: *The Use of the Transfer . . .,* p. 143.

during this period, showed only an occasional success, and usually this "success" was accomplished by environmental manipulation such as a move from the city to the farm. At this time it often was only after long periods of casework that some clients were recognized and diagnosed as "psychopaths."

CLIENT PARTICIPATION: Casework procedure was directed toward the possibility of making the family increasingly more responsible for its own "plan-making." Families were expected to participate and to feel responsible for working out a suggested plan or to substitute a better one. It was believed client participation created more self-reliance on the part of the client.

Treatment Goals

DEFINING TREATMENT: During the last decade and the early part of the twenties, treatment goals in social casework were not clearly defined. Friendly visitors went into the home and helped the sick to obtain medical treatment. They attempted to find work for those who could work and gave financial assistance to those in need. Casework consisted of the "investigation" and this meant emphasis on obtaining the facts of the case. Studies of case records, however, revealed there were facts and problems besides material ones. In the past, casework treatment had consisted of persuading the family that the caseworker's proposal coupled with a periodical review of the situation was the best plan of care. Later in this decade the merits of this kind of treatment were questioned.

Psychiatry and psychology were contributing some knowledge of the client's psychological problems but there was no well-defined casework treatment for the client's psychological problems. Caseworkers believed that coping with the attitudes and the prejudices of individuals was the most difficult task they had to meet. In 1923, Gordon Hamilton predicted more scientific diagnosis and evaluation in casework but did not mention treatment.[1]

By 1925, the goals of treatment were being directed to meeting the client on his own ground, seeing his problem—as much as pos-

---

[1] Gordon Hamilton: Progress in social casework, *The Family*, IV, July, 1923, p. 111.

sible—from his point of view, and helping but not forcing him to a solution of his problem. What had been referred to as "causes" were now being looked upon as "symptoms." It was not until the end of the twenties that emphasis shifted from investigation and diagnosis to defining treatment methods.

EXECUTIVE-LEADERSHIP PLAN: During the twenties, Porter Lee developed what he called the Executive-leadership plan of treatment. He stated that the *Executive* aspect of social treatment involved the discovery of particular resources and the arrangement for the use of them. This type of treatment focused on helping clients find jobs, receive medical treatment, place children in school, and obtain better housing. Executive treatment was also referred to as environmental manipulation.

The *Leadership* aspect of social treatment involved the influence of what he referred to as the personality of the social worker on the client rather than the use of resources. Casework that involved using the Leadership aspect was directed to reconstructing the point of view, or changing the attitude of a client. How workers were accomplishing this was not known as the case records had not, up to this point, given any clue as to how this was being done. Porter Lee stated: "We have long been familiar with these treatment methods [Executive and Leadership] but they have not been discussed, defined, studied, and made available for conscious selection."[1]

Later during this period, the Executive-Leadership goals of treatment were criticized as not usable. There appeared to be few forms of treatment in which Executive aspects without Leadership aspects could be used; that is, these two aspects of treatment could not be separated.

TREATMENT TRENDS FOR CHILDREN: By 1926, there was renewed interest in an old premise in the treatment of children. The goals were to help "make the home fit for the child" instead of removing the child from the home. The belief was that there were hundreds of children in orphanages and foster homes who should or could have remained in their own homes.

---

[1] Porter R. Lee: A study of social treatment, *The Family,* IV, December, 1923, p. 194.

SUMMARY OF THE 1920'S

Social Change

The period of the twenties was characterized by prosperous times and an improved standard of living largely traceable to the expanding economy of World War I. This meant an increase in numbers of the well-to-do, resulting in a still more marked distinction between the wealthy and the poor. The persistent thinking that economic problems could be settled by business alone meant long work hours for little pay to the employed. The shift in relief giving from the municipal level to private agencies brought about continued efforts to differentiate between those who were poor for economic reasons and those who were dependent for physical reasons.

The socio-economic changes of this period resulted in changes in the family. One significant change that occurred was the emancipation of women with the consequent passing of male dominance and lessening of respect for the male's authority as the head of the household. Fathers were increasingly being gainfully employed outside the home which meant that mothers were assuming more of the responsibilities of disciplining the children.

The Family

The family was now seen as a social institution with eight functions and as a "transmitter of the gains of the ages." There was some indication during this period that some of the eight functions of the family were being taken over by other institutions.

The Caseworker

The unpaid friendly visitor of the last decade was now a paid caseworker with some formal training. Trained caseworkers were working with both the client's material problems and his attitudes and prejudices. The focus was on the client's social relations, and caseworkers began to analyze "why they did what they did" in their search for procedures, techniques, and treatment methods.

A fast growing body of knowledge about casework was being developed by workers through statistical and case study research methods. A major contribution from psychiatry was the relating of normal and abnormal behavior. To caseworkers this meant people were no longer considered to have been "born that way."

Casework

The casework focus was on social relations. This meant a shift from "knowing all about a person" to "knowing the person." With more emphasis on the client's point of view, treatment in casework moved from the caseworker's plan to more participation by the client and to more recognition of the client's ability to work out his own plan. Thus, a casework method developed which emphasized leaving the problem in the hands of the client but diagnosing his difficulty.

ILLUSTRATION

OUTLINE FOR RECORDING AND ANALYZING INTERVIEWS

Purpose (when interview was previously planned, include in Interview rather than in Discussion)

Physical Setting (home, office, persons present)

Approach (may include manner, rapport, motivation)

Rapport (making friendly contact)

    Revealing one's interest

    Putting interviewee at ease

    Tying up with interviewee's past experience

    Letting interviewee feel that he is leading interview

    Using colloquial language

Development of Interview

    Coping with Attitude (definition of attitude: "the elements of an attitude are thinking, feeling, wishing, conditioned by early experience"):

        Allowing release of emotions

        Dealing with fears

        Meeting of objections

        Presenting of facts to get certain response

Contradiction
Promises
Presenting impossible plan
Letting interviewee present own plan
Exaggeration of interviewee's suggestions
Reassurance
Interplay between personalities other than interviewer
   and interviewee
Reasoning
Contrasting plans
Informing
Consideration of difficulties
Presenting a possible solution
Compromising
Planning
Turning Point (indicates crisis in conversation which may not
   be marked but always occurs)
Motivation (definition: inciting action)
Use of Incentives:
   Appeal to prejudices:
      (a) Personal
      (b) Group, racial, national, religious, political, la-
           bor, social clubs, etc.
   Interests
   Ambitions
   Pride
   Ideals
   Weaknesses
   Desires
   Tastes
   Esthetic sense
   Sentiment
   Sense of humor
   Sense of justice
   Altruism
Use of Comparisons
Recognition, evaluation, and utilization of new material ap-
   pearing in course of interview

Practical action of interviewer
Obtaining interviewee's help in details
Presentation of final question
Clinching with definite suggestions
Leaving something for interviewee to do

Discussion of Technique (definition of technique: "the style of performance in any art"): The discussion is an analysis, interpretation, and synthesis of the interviewer's method and the interviewee's reactions. It should trace the development of rapport, indicate the ways in which the interviewee's attitude was dealt with and the interviewee motivated. The factors which caused the turning point and which subsequently brought about the change or lack of change in interviewee's point of view should be stressed. In considering the effects and results, the following points should be brought out:

(1) Show effect of interviewer's interest. For example, did it make interviewee talk more freely, flatter his ego, make him feel important?

(2) Indicate the attitudes in interviewee which interfered with interviewer's establishing rapport and gaining free discussion of the difficulties.

(3) Indicate reasons for and results of following interviewee's cues. For example, is it a means of showing interest, getting new facts, learning interviewee's attitudes? Does it make interviewee feel effective and assured?

(4) Show not only the effect of presentation of facts but also the result. For example, does it give interviewee insight into her situation as a whole and take account of factors she had overlooked?

(5) Does appeal to incentives and coping with attitude result in making interviewee feel more effective, assured, over-assured, ineffective, more diffident, etc.?

(6) Did the interviewer persuade the interviewee to take over without modification the plan the former had in mind?

(7) Did the interviewer bring interviewee to compromise somewhat on his own plan; or did interviewer agree to compromise on hers?

(8) Did the two between them think out a plan of action which embodied the best ideas of both but which was different from what either would have thought of alone?

(9) Did the interview leave the situation worse than it was before (it would never be the same as before) —the interviewee angry, or suspicious, or stubborn?

EXPLANATION OF OUTLINE

The *main* headings in the outline are to be noted in the margin opposite the phase of the interview indicated. The *subheadings* in the outline give suggestions for its use and also include various kinds of technique involved in case work interviewing. These terms are merely suggestions for use in the Discussion of Technique only, and need not appear in the margin. The list is tentative and incomplete—any other methods used by the worker in her interviews should be added. The marginal notes are merely a guide in reading the record; the discussion is an analysis of the worker's technique and the psychological results with the interviewee. It appears as a separate paragraph following the interview. The illustrative interview[1] shows the use of the outline. The situation is given to make the interview clear as an illustration and is not necessary to put in the record.

ILLUSTRATIVE INTERVIEW

Joseph, an unstable boy of thirteen, considered by the psychiatrist in danger of developing a psychosis unless removed from his home, had spent part of his summer vacation on a farm. Consent had been obtained from both parents to allow him to spend the winter. Although the home is inadequate there is no question of immorality, so that court action is not possible and foster care for Joseph depends entirely on the parents' co-operation. However,

---

[1] Interview by Annette M. Garrett, United Charities of Chicago.

his father is a suspicious, evasive Greek and his mother is an hysterical woman of very low grade intelligence and no sense of truthfulness so that no decision is easy to gain or possible to consider final. She has repeatedly demanded Joseph's return in spite of the fact that previously she had readily consented to the plan.

During the past winter without the worker's knowledge, his father had enrolled Joseph in a course in mechanics in a pay school. By the school record it was shown that he attended irregularly throughout the term and his scholarship was low. The superintendent advised that although the school admits students of any age, Joseph was too young to profit by the course of lectures which is the only thing open to first year pupils.

INTERVIEW

October 7, 1925
Physical Setting

Mrs. Mores came to the office at 1:30 with Paul. She was very angry and glowered at the worker. She first handed worker a letter from Joseph. Worker jokingly asked her if she didn't like to have him eating apples off the tree. Paul interpreted that it's all right for a person to go away for a two weeks' vacation, but not to stay all winter. There was a great deal of excited conversation about $55 invested in the Dane School, and that Joseph was to

Manner of Interviewee
Manner of Interviewer
Rapport

come back so as not to waste that money, and that the children had to stay away from school today because they had no shoes, because they had spent all their money on the school. The worker offered to ask for School Children's Aid shoes but Mrs. Mores refused angrily. Over and over again she excitedly demanded Joseph's return, and insisted that if he is not back by the end of the week she will go after him.

Presently the worker engaged Paul in conversation about himself, his school, and George. Then he was asked about his stay in

the country. His face beamed as he talked about the good time
he had, but when he was asked if he would not like to stay there

Manner of Interviewee

all winter he answered, in the same words that he had interpreted
for his mother earlier, "It's all right to stay for two weeks, but not
all winter." However, he did not appear to believe this very sin-
cerely. Mrs. Mores sat glowering during this conversation and
when the talk was allowed to revert back to Joseph she remarked
that her real reason for wanting him back was because Mr. Mores
insisted on his coming back to go to Dane School. The worker,

Coping with Attitude

assuming that this was true, said, "That's right, Mrs. Mores, you
tell me the truth about it and we can work out some way together,
I am sure, to give Joseph this splendid chance. If Mr. Mores tells
you that Joseph can go back to Dane School, he is mistaken because that money has all been used up long ago and they will not
take him back unless another $50 is paid. When you pay your milk
bill in advance two months of course they won't go on delivering
milk four months." This had been said before when Mrs. Mores
was excitedly demanding his return, but it did not have any effect

Motivation

until now. Then the worker told her that Joseph is in 8B, that he
has an ex-school teacher to help him every night with his lessons
and that if she leaves him there he will graduate.. While she was
insisting that he had been in the 8th grade in Chicago, the worker
jokingly remarked that she knew he had not come within a mile of
the 7th grade and would never graduate in Chicago, because he
will not go to day school, and he is too young to get along in Dane
School. At this point the worker was called to the telephone.

Turning Point

When she returned after ten minutes Paul interpreted, "My mother says Joseph should stay out there where he can graduate from

school and have a teacher help him with his lessons every night and not be bumming around here on the streets and getting into trouble stealing, and that if my father beats her she'll hide under the house and that scares him because he thinks she is going to leave him." Mrs. Mores still sat soberly by. The worker took her hand and enthusiastically shook it, exclaiming, "That's the way to talk, that's fine. Now we'll stick together and see that Joseph has a chance to graduate and learns to be self-supporting, so that he can help you at home." Mrs. Mores' face was all smiles and after a few minutes the worker asked her to come upstairs and see the children in kindergarten. They were asleep. Mrs. Mores tiptoed about interestedly, saying over and over again, "it's just like a hospital," and as soon as she was out in the hall she asked if she could bring the children. Then she asked for suggestions about work, saying that she is so used to working that she does not like

Motivation

to stay at home. Mr. Mores has spent all the money buying all the fruit and vegetables he canned, and now it's too early to sell them and so they have not any money. When she was saying she was afraid her husband would get a divorce if she insisted upon Joseph's staying away and the worker said, "Oh he wouldn't do that after all these years," Paul said, "Yes he would, my mother looks old, she's had so many children and works so hard, and he's a young looking man, he doesn't look over 25."

Then the worker told Mrs. Mores how badly Joseph needs clothes and asked if she could not send his sweater. She was anxious to send it but knew that her husband would not let her. Evidently she arranged with Paul in Greek that he would pretend to lose the sweater, for presently she announced that she would send the sweater into the office within the next few days and winked at Paul. Then she offered to send a good tailored coat which she had gotten from Community Center for Josephine last year, and a sweater. She wanted to wash the sweater though, and when she thought of that she became very impatient to get home and get at it.

DISCUSSION OF TECHNIQUE

The interview was unpremeditated and so had no planned purpose except that the conscious purpose of the worker for weeks had been to persuade the family to let Joseph remain in the country. The worker first sparred for time, seizing upon parts of the letter which could not possibly be objected to—attempting to break through Mrs. Mores' negativism. There was no outward indication that this was successful and Mrs. Mores was allowed to purge her mind. Her objections and complaints poured forth and the worker constantly tried to meet them or redirect them. Although unsuccessful in guiding the conversation, the effect of catharsis was showing faintly in that Mrs. Mores could not keep up quite such a rapid torrent of words. Feeling that further argument was useless, the worker engaged Paul in conversation which could not be regarded unfavorably by Mrs. Mores, yet ignored her temporarily. This also was a kind of catharsis, giving her time to let her anger drain off in silence. From this time on the interview moved forward. The worker had control. Mrs. Mores' objections could now be accepted as sincere and an attempt made to meet them by reasoning and presenting of facts which earlier would not have been heard. A practical comparison about the milk bill was used. The real turning point came with the response to the worker's presentation of the facts about Joseph's possibilities of school success. This appealed to racial pride and an ideal, and, at least for the present, Mrs. Mores was won over. The worker seized upon her temporary abandonment of negativism to make her actively do things. She was shown the nursery, not because getting the children there was the immediate goal, but because she had before refused to come near it or let herself be interested. Finally she was left with something to do, not because of the worth of Joseph's old clothes which she might gather up, but because by so doing she was actively taking a part in keeping him there, not just grudgingly giving her consent.[1]

---

[1] Helen L. Myrick: Psychological processes in interviewing, *The Family*, VII, March, 1926, pp. 26-28.

REFERENCES

Books

Richmond, Mary: *What is Social Casework?* New York, Russell Sage Foundation, 1922.

Articles

Blackman, Elinor: Some tests for the evaluation of case work methods, *The Family, VI:* 5:132-137, July 1925.

Blanchard, Phyllis, and Paynter, Richard H.: Socio-psychological status of children from marginal families, *The Family, VIII:* 1:3-10, March 1927.

Brisley, Mary S.: An attempt to articulate processes, *The Family, V:* 6:157-161, October 1924.

Bruno, Frank J.: Family social work, *The Family, VI:* 5:141-145, July 1925.

_____' The meaning of the conference, *The Family, VIII:* 8:261-269, December 1927.

_____: Understanding human nature, *The Family, VIII:* 2:58-60, April 1927.

Buell, Bradley: Interviews, interviewers, *The Family, VI:* 3:86-90, May 1925.

Burgess, Ernest W.: The family as a unity of interacting personalities, *The Family, VII:* 1:3-9, March 1926.

Dexter, Elizabeth H.: The social case worker's attitude and problems as they affect her work, *The Family, VII:* 6:177-195, October 1926.

Dunham, Arthur: The elements of a successful social service exchange, *The Family, III:* 10:240-243, February 1923.

Everett, Edith: Helping fathers and mothers to be better parents, *The Family, IV:* 5:121-126, July 1923.

Hamilton, Gordon: Progress in social case work, *The Family, IV:* 5:111-118, July 1923.

Hanchette, Helen W.: Home economics as a working force in family casework, *The Family, II:* 5:111-116, July 1921.

Healy, William: The application of mental tests in family casework, *The Family, II:* 5:97-100, July 1921.

Hewins, Katherine P.: Division of responsibility between family and children's agencies, *The Family, III:* 7:177-180, November 1922.

Hill, Lewis: A psychiatrist's notes on family case work problems, *The Family, X:* 8:241-247, December 1929.

Hurlbutt, Mary E.: The invisible environment of an immigrant, *The Family*, IV: 6:160-164, October 1923.

Jocher, Katherine: Methods of research in studying the family, *The Family*, IX: 3:80-85, May 1928.

Kahn, Dorothy C.: The need for interpretation of trends and accomplishments in family social work, *The Family*, VIII: 5: 148-153, July 1927.

Karpf, Maurice J.: Relation of length of treatment to improvement or adjustment of social case work problems, *The Family*, VIII: 5:144-148, July 1927.

Kempton, Helen P.: Skill in casework, *The Family*, IX: 8:260-263, December 1928.

————: The class teaches itself, *The Family*, X: 2:49-56, April 1929.

Lee, Porter R.: A study of social treatment, *The Family*, IV: 8:191-199, December 1923.

————: Changes in social thought and standards which affect the family, *The Family*, IV: 5:103-111, July 1923.

Libbey, Betsey: The approach of the case worker in the family agency, *The Family*, V: 5:118-121, July 1924.

Lucas, Jean M.: The interview of persuasison, *The Family*, V: 5:128-132, July 1924.

Luric, H. L.: Specialized approaches to family case work, *The Family*, VIII: 6:202-205, October 1927.

Lynde, Edward D.: The significance of changing methods in relief giving, *The Family*, VIII: 5:135-144, July 1927.

Myrick, Helen L.: Psychological processes in interviewing, *The Family*, VII: 1:25-29, March 1926.

Phelps, Harold A.: The case record and scientific method, *The Family*, VIII: 4:103-109, June 1927.

Raymond, Stockton: The responsibility of a family agency at a time of industrial readjustment, *The Family*, II: 5:121-124, July 1921.

Relief not needed, *The Family*, I: 8:16-17, May 1920.

Review of: What is social casework? by Mary E. Richmond, *The Family*, III: 3:69-70, May 1922.

Richmond, Mary: Some next steps in social treatment, *The Family*, I: 4:6-10, June 1920.

————: Some relations of family casework to social progress, *The Family*, III: 5:99-104, July 1922.

Riley, Thomas J.: Teaching household management, *The Family, III:* 1:13-17, March 1922.

Robinson, Virginia P.: Analysis of processes in the records of family case working agencies, *The Family, II:* 5:101-106, July 1921.

Salsberry, Pearl: Techniques in case work, *The Family, VIII:* 5:153-157, July 1927.

Skolsky, Anna F.: A recreational approach to family casework, *The Family, X:* 4:107-109, June 1929.

Taft, Jessie: The effect of an unsatisfactory mother-daughter relationship upon the development of a personality, *The Family, VII:* 1:10-17, March 1926.

——————: The problems of casework with children, *The Family, I:* 5:1-8, July 1920.

——————: The spirit of social work, *The Family, IX:* 4:103-107, June 1928.

——————: The relation of psychology to social work, *The Family, VII:* 7:199-203, November 1926.

——————: The use of the transfer within the limits of the office interview, *The Family, V:* 6:143-146, October 1924.

The Co-operation of relatives, *The Family, II:* 7:163-167, November 1921.

Vlachos, Anna: Opening the way, *The Family, V:* 6:153-157, October 1924.

Wickendon, Homer: Examples of casework treatment, *The Family, I:* 7:24-25, November 1920.

Wilcox, Ellen F.: The measurement of achievement in family casework, *The Family, VIII:* 2:46-49, April 1927.

Woodberry, Laura: The modern case work exchange, *The Family, V:* 3:51-56, May 1924.

Chapter III

THE DEPRESSION, DECADE 1930-1939

The greatest task before civilization at present is to make machines what they ought to be, the slaves, instead of the masters of men.

HAVELOCK ELLIS *(1859-1939)*

SOCIAL CHANGE

The Depression, Economics and the Family

THE MAJOR social change in the period 1930-1939 was the wholesale replacement of men by machines which in turn contributed to nationwide problem of unemployment. The depression period found voluntary agencies unable to carry the financial burden of the unemployed. The attitude of the general public was that this serious problem of unemployment was beyond the control of the individual and of private agencies, and that resolutions for the problem must come from the industrial and economic fields.

A study of fifty families conducted during the thirties revealed that practically all were in a condition of semi-starvation, were unable to pay rent or insurance, and none were receiving assistance due to the exhausted funds of private agencies. The most significant finding of the study was the identification of family solidarity as a major force—a "united-in-a-common-cause-and-still-fighting" spirit. A second significant finding of the study was the discovery of the terrific price most families were willing to pay to keep their children with them.

During these depression years families withstood conditions and calamities which, in the more protective phase of casework practice, it was not believed a family could withstand. At this time many agencies were engaged in a serious struggle to meet the financial needs of their clients.

Research revealed that in Chicago, in 1930, voluntary agencies were carrying only about 40 per cent of the relief burden and that there were periodic "closed doors" because of insufficient funds. By 1932, the relief giving burden carried by private agencies in that city was reduced to 10 per cent. *This significant change occurred throughout the entire country and was the result of a shift in relief giving from private agencies to the government.*

Even though voluntary agencies could not meet the financial needs of their clients, they were determined that this need must be met. They contributed to the public welfare agencies that were being established by the government by supplying methods, routines, and procedures, standards of relief, staff competence and budget principles. A number of competent workers in the employ of private agencies were drafted by rapidly developing public welfare relief and state unemployment departments. This caused drastic changes in the services private agencies were offering to clients. Differences arose between public and private services which were not readily settled.

By 1933, the depression and the unemployment problems had brought about definite changes in the practice of social casework. The *individual approach* to the troubles of human lives, fitting the help given to the need of the client, was now being carried out independent of the giving of relief and the accumulation of unnecessary data. Linton Swift wrote:

> Most of us have long recognized in theory that we should not have to give relief for unemployment or to supplement wages. The trouble is that it remained a beautiful theory, but as a working principle it was relegated usually to the distant future. And to the extent to which such unsocial relief is gradually removed from our budget we shall not only remedy our financial difficulties but we shall also be able to do better casework with families whose distress is due to internal causes rather than general economic conditions.[1]

Less emphasis was placed on the economic aspects of the helping process as a result of the inability of caseworkers to meet the

---

[1] Linton B. Swift: The relief problem in family social work, *The Family*, X, March, 1929, p. 3.

financial needs of clients. Financial assistance was used to help
clients meet crisis situations and to conserve the family values.
Relief giving in itself was no longer a major function but was used
as an aid in exploring the motivation and the desire of the client
to accept casework services. With the curtailment of economic
assistance to clients, the stigma of accepting help for personal
problems decreased. Caseloads in the thirties included the white
collar class who were seeking help with the problem of accepting
their current situations. Other clients came from the "under-
world" and included petty thieves, bootleggers, prostitutes and
gangsters. These changes in caseloads caused caseworkers to
re-evaluate their own feelings; and as they became more accepting, they tended to discard their former moralistic attitudes.

The many changes in casework services gave rise to a change in
the thinking of the general public. Prior to this time, the public
had thought that the function of the caseworker was mainly the
giving of relief. Caseworkers feared that the public would not
support agencies other than those which gave relief. One writer
stated: "Therein [public support] lies the supreme test for a new
evaluation of casework . . . a challenge to us, from which new
strengths may be developed for an enrichment of family life and
for the strengthening of our profession."[1]

THE FAMILY

Social Change and the Family

The social changes of this era brought alterations in the family.
The "modern" family of the thirties emerged as the product of the
loss or serious constriction of many of the eight functions of the
family that existed in the twenties. The economic functions of the
family had been ceded to the factory, store, and office. Family
status, to a marked degree, was lost in what was considered an age
of mobility and large cities. Approximately half of the educational
functions of the family were transferred to the schools. Religion
had lost a measure of its influence in family matters; and most

---

[1] John P. Sanderson: The family society of tomorrow, *The Family*, XIV, April, 1933,
p. 43.

recreation was sought outside the home in moving picture theaters, parks, city streets, and clubs. Police and social legislation largely removed the protective functions from the home to the state. This left only two family functions, that of giving affection and also reproduction. A significant outcome of the transfer of functions from the family to outside institutions was a marked decline in the authority of the family. Increasing authority was being assumed by state and industry which lessened the authority within the institution of the family.

THE CASEWORKER

Problem Solving

During this age of unemployment, caseworkers were faced with an overwhelming number of applicants seeking aid. They were unable to investigate or obtain all the factual data necessary for each application. They were, therefore, forced to assume that the statements made by the client were correct. In addition, they felt that they should not add to the burden of the client by presenting an attitude that suggested mistrust. Caseworkers were now more inclined to give the client the benefit of the doubt.

Helping clients readjust to lowered income posed complex problems. Caseworkers needed a working knowledge of housing conditions, rental rates and food costs in order to assist the family to budget their income. Homemaker services were provided and available health facilities were utilized.

What was occasionally referred to as the reticence or passivity of caseworkers in the interviewing situation was now recognized as actually due to "a greater control of the caseworker's own curiosity" and "impulse to save." Caseworkers were less active in the interview thus permitting an "activation of healing self-knowledge" in the client. Clients were viewed as having the ability to discuss their problems and to sort out those factors which were external from those which were within themselves.

From their casework experience, caseworkers were learning that they should not criticize, blame or condemn the behavior of the individual nor should they put their own feelings, expressed or unexpressed, in the way of the client's freedom to express his. There was a greater recognition of the fact that to bring about change a client needs to want to change. As Florence Day wrote:

> I do think we are trying very hard not to impose our opinions or even subtle influences into our clients decisions, but we do have subjective inclinations in one direction or another, and I believe a conscious looking at what they might be will put us more completely in control so that they will not creep out unexpectedly.[1]

Caseworkers were not giving sympathy but empathy and understanding in the client-caseworker relationship. They believed the client needed to "experience" this understanding and interest, and that the client would respond not only to the spoken words of the caseworker but the total impression of her personality in this relationship. They felt that in order to change human behavior, it must first be understood.

> If we want people to feel understood, then it is necessary to become a person who does understand. If we want clients to give us their confidence, we have to become people who inspire confidence. It cannot be just a matter of verbal acrobatics, or unassimilated methods and techniques.[2]

Caseworkers saw the clients' symptoms as an attempt to effect a solution of their problems, and they were seeing the clients' behavior as a means of "blocking" the process of meeting basic conscious and unconscious needs. *Caseworkers were now relating the client's social and personal adjustment to capacities and wishes of the client and not to an ideal standard.*

Marriage Counseling

Caseworkers grew more definitive as they were drawn into counseling services of couples with marital problems. No at-

---

[1] Florence R. Day: Changing practices in casework treatment, *The Family,* XVIII, March, 1937, p. 6.

[2] Florence T. Waite: A little matter of self-respect, *The Family,* XVII, March, 1936, p. 12.

tempt was made to "fix the blame" for the difficulty the spouses were experiencing, but there was an effort to understand the problem by exploring the partners' attitudes and the events leading to the discord. Assistance with marital problems involved careful interviewing with close and regular contacts which often continued over a period of years. Attempts were made to classify marital discord into two types: (1) those of personality disorganization and where the marriage relationship constituted an additional conflict; (2) the conflicts arising out of the marriage situation itself including sexual, cultural, health, or economic problems. There were times when caseworkers felt that all they could expect to do was to "stand by the spouses" and to help guide them in the process of thinking through their marital problems as a means of enabling them to gain a better understanding of themselves in relation to other members of their family.

Family Centered Casework

The major problem of the family during the years 1930-1939 was poverty. Families were seeking help in coping with their poverty and the resultant complications. Caseworkers were interpreting to families: (a) the many meanings of the tensions which built up in the family due to unemployment, and (b) that personality disintegration was often caused by a new and strange way of living. Research studies at this time intensified a belief that it was the client's right to work out his own life in his own way.[1] Caseworkers were viewing *their rights* as limited to the control of what they gave of themselves as helping persons, and the use of resources available to clients. They were no longer attempting to "protect" the client or to make life easy for him by doing things to him or for him. Caseworkers, restricted financially and physically overworked, were, despite this strain, expected to give casework services to family members with delicacy and respect for human personality.

Bertha Reynolds, in discussing Virginia P. Robinson's book, *A Changing Psychology in Social Casework*, stated, "The ultimate

---

[1] Marjorie Boggs: Family social work in relation to family life, *The Family*, XV, July, 1934, p. 146.

goal [in social casework] is to develop in the individual the fullest possible capacity for self-maintenance in a social group."[1] Continued studies of case histories strengthened the caseworkers' confidence in the client's capacity for self-help when given the opportunity to discover his own strengths. *The observation during the thirties that individuals and families could withstand overwhelming odds brought to light family strengths and added new dimensions to family centered casework.*

Specialization

As social workers entered medical and psychiatric settings, the trend in social work education increasingly turned to specialized training. Bertha Reynolds questioned this trend and wondered if casework was becoming a "relationship therapy," with emotionally sick persons. She stated that caseworker and client should know when the caseworker is acting as therapist and when as caseworker.[2] By 1939, the focus in social work education slowly shifted back to a more generic casework approach, but the focus on the clients' internal problems continued into the next decade.

Up to this time the casework field was mainly staffed by women, but during the thirties men began to enter the field of social work as caseworkers. Caseworkers carried smaller caseloads which made it possible to devote more time, understanding, and privacy to the client's problem.

Research

The two methods of social research, the *statistical* and the *case study* developed in the twenties, saw more widespread use in the thirties. The *statistical method* was quantitative and dealt with objective facts that could be clearly enumerated and measured. The *case study method* dealt with qualitative non-numerical data. The case study which did not permit generalization was now considered indispensable to the understanding of a human

---

[1] Bertha C. Reynolds: A changing psychology in social casework, *The Family,* XII, June, 1931, p. 109.

[2] *Ibid.*

situation and was being used in treatment planning. Both of these research plans were supplementary to each other as each method had a valid function to perform.

The development of a scoring system to measure or evaluate movement in casework was in progress. First, problem syndromes had to be identified. Then, scores were worked out on the basis of such criteria as *adjustment, credit, merit* and *tempo*. Adjustment referred to the client; credit referred to how much recognition the agency could assume for the client's adjustment; merit referred to the technique, skill and judgment in treatment of the problem, and tempo dealt with the promptness and intensity of the services being given.[1]

Psychiatry and the Caseworker

Through the contributions made by the field of psychiatry, caseworkers were obtaining a better understanding of the occurrence and the use of "transference" in casework. Lucille Austin referred to the transference as a "reaction to a person or situation not only stimulated by the immediate situation, but also conditioned by an earlier emotional experience, particularly that of childhood."[2] Otto Rank's *Will Psychology*, which was organized around the concept of the "ego," was also being incorporated into the caseworker's knowledge.[3] With increased involvement of caseworkers in working with clients' internal problems, some private agencies began to employ psychiatrists as consultants to caseworkers on individual cases.

Professional Vocabulary

Words such as principles, philosophy, concepts, methods, and process, were from time to time used interchangeably. The prob-

---

[1] Ellery F. Reed: The classification of case work problems, *The Family*, VI, May, 1930, p. 83-85.

[2] Lucille Austin: The evolution of our social casework concepts, *The Family*, XX, April, 1939, p. 47.

[3] Grace F. Marcus: Some implications for casework of Rank's psychology, *The Family*, XVIII, December, 1937, p. 274.

lem of semantics remained virtually unsolved since terms such as attitude therapy, psychological therapy, relationship therapy, depth therapy, executive treatment, and casework counseling were felt to be incomplete formulations. It was also believed that these terms needed to be exposed to the "tempering of experience" to lend more sureness and preciseness to their use.

CASEWORK

General Methods

IDENTIFYING THE NEED: Clients were being helped to recognize that there were factors other than financial in their situation and the focus changed from sustained to temporary relief giving. Clients were given assistance in planning for the future so that continued relief would not be necessary.

In the early thirties, first interviews were attempts to determine whether the need of the applicant rose purely from his unemployment or whether his need was far deeper. In many cases the client had only a hazy notion of the services he might seek from an agency or where he could turn for help. It was felt that initial interviews with clients demanded considerable experience, skill, resourcefulness and evaluative ability of the caseworker. As early as 1930, Grace Marcus pointed out that sensitive handling of the initial contact should be an intrinsic part of casework. It was beginning to be recognized that not all clients who asked for help wanted their problems studied and treated.

> We may study a problem carefully but we do not take it up formally as a responsibility until we are sure the client is able or willing to work on it. Our casework position is that the client always has the right to decide whether he wants help on the terms we feel are the only terms for intelligently helping him. We respect this right of the client to decide even when his attitude precludes our assisting him.[1]

EXTERNAL AND INTERNAL CASEWORK FACTORS: External or environmental factors referred to "manipulation of the client's set-

---

[1] Grace F. Marcus: Some tentative methods of adjusting case loads, *The Family*, XI, October, 1930, p. 188.

ting," the use of special resources, offering of general education and the client's use of social opportunities. Internal factors meant working with the emotional needs and attitudes of the client. These two general methods were also referred to as "indirect" and "direct" casework. One of the most perplexing difficulties which beset caseworkers arose from the fact that often both the client and the social situation were in stages of disequilibrium, or "upset." As a consequence, it was difficult to differentiate between interacting causes and effects. It was equally difficult to ascertain whether external or internal factors were dominant and which was the most susceptible to modification.

DIFFERENTIAL DIAGNOSIS: By 1936, Florence Hollis stated "We were very close to the spread of 'therapy' in casework. Everyone wanted to be a therapist and there was a feeling of apology if one's skill lay in environmental readjustment."[1]

By 1939, caseworkers were no longer attempting to differentiate between the client's internal and external problems. The client's past and present experiences, other people who had influenced him, his feelings and attitudes were all incorporated into the caseworker's thinking. The client's relationship to the worker in the interview was considered only one force. *This thoughtful and analytical consideration of evidence from many sources was referred to as differential diagnosis.*[2]

OFFICE INTERVIEWS: In contrast to the decade of the twenties when whole families were treated, one member of the family was being singled out as the client in the thirties. If two members of the family needed treatment, the second member was assigned to another caseworker. The initial interview involved exploring the client's capacity to enter into a participating relationship with the caseworker in meeting and treating his problems. Although caseworkers saw clients on an individual basis, the firm base on which they planned to proceed was individual casework in the area of working with the needs and problems of families and how these could be met. *By 1934, intake interviews were permanently es-*

1 Florence Hollis: Individualized service to families in the private agency, *The Family*, XIX, October, 1938, p. 187.

2 Austin: *op. cit.*, p. 48.

tablished. Emphasis was placed on the application being made by the client and in the office, in preference to home visits.

SUPERVISION: Caseworkers were using their supervisors as freely as clients used the caseworkers. Supervisors were used to modify conflicts over a situation and alter adverse or improper attitudes toward clients. Through the use of supervision, caseworkers were able to move from intolerance to tolerance of certain forms of conduct and finally toward an understanding which was considered to be neither tolerance nor intolerance.

Procedure and Techniques

THE INTERVIEW: The interview had specific purposes and closely followed the lead of the client. It was not a routine procedure nor was it used to "check on the client." The attitude assumed by the caseworker, therefore, had to be one of sympathetic acceptance of the problems which the client wished to discuss. In addition, the caseworker needed to have an awareness of those difficulties the client withheld from direct discussion but which the client implied by his use of words and actions.

As awareness of the inter-relationship of the social study and the treatment processes developed, recognition was given to the diagnostic value of the client's subjective feelings. These were often of more concern to him than his external situation or the objective facts. The decision of whether to offer the client the "therapy of environmental change" or direct treatment of his inner emotional disturbances was dependent primarily on his need and his desire for help. If the client saw the solution of his difficulty only in a change of situation and if such a change were possible, it was considered best to try the client's plan.

By 1936, caseworkers were giving up the systematic explorations or investigations they had been conducting because the data was found to furnish no valid diagnosis for practical use. Information about the client's past, they felt, often estranged caseworker and client from the present and "dynamic relationship." Factual data was obtained from clients only because of the significance it had for the client.

> If it is our desire to fortify others by building up their self-esteem we defeat our own ends when on first acquaintance we seek to uncover their past and send them out feeling as though they had left behind their spiritual clothing. An individual is released from pressure when he voluntarily puts into words the things that trouble him, but his self-esteem is enhanced when he is allowed the privilege of reticence at points where he is unwilling or unable to reveal himself.[1]

The investigation was now believed to be "antipsychological" in procedure.

More skill in the use of the interview was viewed as an aid in therapy. Caseworkers were seen as involved in the "personality development" of the client, and they were expected to give clients some explanation of their emotional conflicts.

THE TOTAL PERSON: The process of combining relief giving with individual treatment became a subject of controversy. As the client became a party to the procedure of problem solving, the trend in casework was to work with the client's attitudes as they appeared in relation to his difficulties. Commonly identified attitudes were feelings of anxiety about work adjustment, about re-employment, or in regard to health. The client's conflicts, such as lack of self-confidence or lack of ability to do a job, were exposed and discussed. It was found that helping clients to express their "ambivalent feelings" lessened anxiety and enabled them to assume more responsibility for their own decisions. Personality disintegration was often markedly reduced by helping the client to take care of his own needs and meet his own responsibilities.

Formerly, only the partial needs of the individual and partial reasons for his trouble had been recognized. As more emphasis was placed on differential diagnosis, caseworkers could see clients as "total living, feeling persons" who consciously and unconsciously expressed their troubles in their behavior and words. Caseworkers endeavored to "individualize each client" in his own situation. Individuals were seen as dynamic, ever-changing, feeling, thinking, "total" human beings. *The caseworker's concern was to*

---

[1] Eleanor Neustaedter: The role of the case worker in treatment, *The Family*, XIII, July, 1932, p. 153.

reach the underlying emotional attitudes of clients, their sense of
failure and defeat that might be the real cause of dependency.

CLIENT PARTICIPATION: It was the manner in which the refusal
for relief was handled that brought about a change in casework.
The casework focus was on helping the client face the reality
situation, with special consideration being given to the client's
capacity to use such help. During these depression years, many
unemployed were in need and were refused relief. As a result of
this refusal, the major problem was considered to be the family's
loss of morale. As one writer explained: "We may not be able to
meet his [the client's] material needs, but we can at least build up
a feeling of his own worth by an attitude which suggests belief in
his integrity, respect for his personality, and regret for the situation in which he finds himself."[1] It was considered a truism that
when individuals found their self-esteem threatened they naturally turned to those who offered understanding.

Caseworkers were able to help unemployed clients entangled in
a mesh of circumstances over which they had no control to understand that their problems were recognized and that the situation
was not of their own making.

THE RELATIONSHIP: Casework appeared to be developing in
spirals. This was an era of the *relationship*, of *identification*, and
client participation as caseworker's endeavored to be of use to all
troubled clients. The caseworker's relationship to the client was
now considered to be the most important factor in casework.
Authors were stating that: "Unless the caseworker can create
confidence in himself such that the client chooses to share his
burdens with him [the caseworker] there is no casework service
given or received,"[2] and "To spend two hours in establishing a
partnership relationship is less costly, both in money and time,
than to spend ten minutes in a routine interview."[3] The client-
caseworker relationship involved accepting the client "at his

---

[1] *Ibid.*, p. 147.

[2] Bertha Reynolds: Social casework, what is it? What is its place in the world today?
The Family, XVI, December, 1935, p. 235.

[3] Fern Lowry: Casework skills and fundamental human needs, *The Family,* XIV, July,
1933, p. 159.

worst" just as freely as when he was "at his best." The primary objective was to create confidence in clients, taking care not to do too much or to give what the client could not use.

Clients were given the opportunity constructively to rid themselves of guilt feelings. With the remission of these feelings, there was no longer a fear of punishment and clients were then able to be increasingly honest in revealing feelings of which they had previously been ashamed. Clients were more ready to ask for help with their inner problems when they realized that the caseworker was not going to threaten, approve, rescue or overwhelm them. In the security of professional undestanding, clients were given help in working out a better adjustment to their situation. Caseworkers recognized that their part in the interview required that they not attempt to change the attitude of the client. They saw that people change when they have the feeling that a different type of behavior or activity will be more satisfying. As clients revealed their own needs and determined what use they would make of the caseworker, they were able to work out their problems on their own initiative. It was observed that clients received the most benefit from what they could do for themselves. If the client was not criticized, he respected himself a little more, and as his self-respect developed, his hostility toward himself and others decreased.

The trend was increasingly directed toward defining the caseworker's role with less attention paid to the development of the treatment plan. Caseworkers now saw their role as determined and developed out of the interview, step by step, whereas the client's problem was seen as "being left with the client." Clients were using the client-caseworker relationship according to their needs and desires. This was considered to be a continuous process beginning with the manner in which the initial application was received and ending with the last contact.

As the client became a more mature, adjusted personality able to cope with his own problems, many of his so-called "social problem" disapeared. This was seen as the result of the client's having solved the problem for himself. In the security of the client-caseworker relationship, clients projected less and began to function on their own behalf. Two unifying casework forces were seen as underlying all the separate steps the caseworker and client took together. They were: (1) a search for understanding, and (2) use of that understanding leading to creative action.

Gordon Hamilton, in 1937, stated that casework required sensitivity to people as human beings, and that clients, so far as possible, should be left to manage their own affairs. Opportunities and services were to be made available to clients by consistently using the principles of client activity, client participation, and client consent.[1] *Thus the client-caseworker relationship developed in a unique way in social casework. The relationship, while functioning as a therapeutic force, essentially left the problem in the client's hands but at the same time was instrumental in the diagnosis of his difficulty.*

Treatment Goals

INDIVIDUALIZATION: During the thirties, three major casework treatment forms evolved: (1) use of environmental modifications; (2) use of environmental factors aimed toward affecting individual attitudes and relationships; and (3) working with the client's subjective realities, that is, his emotional conflicts and feelings in order to bring about a better adjustment within himself.[2] Caseworkers recognized the need to observe and accept different levels of adjustment for different people.

Individualization of casework treatment meant accepting different levels of adjustment for different people and fitting the help given to the particular needs of the clients. Treatment could be a matter of active participation and planning with the client in a mutual attempt to overcome difficulties growing out of health problems, or social and economic conditions. It could mean interpretation of social resources of the community available for the benefit of families who had the capacity for self-help but lacked the knowledge of availability and use of resources.

---

1 Gordon Hamilton: Basic concepts in social casework, *The Family*, XVIII, July, 1937, p. 147.

2 *Differential Approach in Casework Treatment*, New York, Family Welfare Association of America, 1936, pp. 4-6.

Problems of the times and the treatment goals that were being used were: (a) In physical illness, the caseworker attempted to stimulate the client's interest in outside affairs as an effort to help prevent chronic illness. (b) Where there were broken families, for example, the father's absence from the home, the caseworker helped the mother with employment problems and helped her to seek other friendships rather than devote all her affection to the children. (c) Clients with thwarted personal ambitions were guided to interests in the community, in the home, and to available intellectual interests. (d) Caseworkers endeavored to recognize psychopathic personalities as it was believed little help could be given them. (e) Marital difficulties involving sexual problems called for "a sane, practical and understanding approach." (f) Problems of alcoholism meant additional care needed to be taken not to undermine the self-respect of the client and attempts should be made to improve conditions inside and outside the home. (g) Where cases of "insanity" were involved, caseworkers felt all they could do was attempt to understand the feelings of inferiority and insecurity of the client and to look at both the hereditary and the social inheritance involved in the problem.

THERAPY: New knowledge of human growth and behavior and the inability to correct "environmental situations" resulting from the depression were significant influences in the trend toward working with the clients' internal problems.

PREVENTIVE APPROACH: With increased skill in psycho-social diagnosis, treatment plans were more specifically spelled out. Intensive treatment was given for behavior problems, for delinquency, to avert the breakup of homes, and problems of deterioration through chronic dependency. Emphasis in casework was placed on helping clients "in time," that is, in the early stages of their trouble. This meant sustaining them through periods of stress, helping them to understand their difficulties and how those difficulties could be met, and providing resources, financial and otherwise, when help was needed.

Casework goals were "the healthiest possible functioning of the individual physically, psychologically and economically in his own social situation."

SUMMARY OF THE 1930'S

Social Change: Social change in the thirties resulted in mass replacement or displacement of men by the machine. Change to the factory system meant that increasing authority was assumed by industry and the state rather than by the family. The major problem of the time was poverty. The magnitude of the unemployment problem and the existing semi-starvation brought a significant change in the shift of the relief-giving function of private agencies to State and Federal government.

The Family: The family, which had experienced serious constriction in all but two of its eight functions, was further constricted in its functions by the social changes of this decade. Families were caught in a struggle to maintain the standard of living acquired during the last decade and their most significant strength was that shown in the struggle to stay together as a family.

The Caseworker: Caseworkers were discarding old moralistic ideas toward the poor and family counseling was now an established part of casework services. Due to the urgency of the problems of the times and the huge number of people involved, there was a shift from family-centered home visits to individual office interviews. The interview became the chief tool of the caseworker. The significance of the *relationship* in the interview meant that caseworkers were moving from intolerance or tolerance to understanding. The casework approach of helping both the client and his social situation was referred to as "differential diagnosis." The caseworkers' efforts directed to building up self-esteem in clients and helping them to face their problems strengthened the caseworkers' confidence in the client's capacity for self-help. Research, now well established, was disclosing syndromes of chronic dependency, broken homes, mental and physical breakdowns, and delinquency.

Casework: The casework principles of considering the total person and client participation were crystalizing. The focus of casework turned to preventive aspects and attempted to reach problems in the early stages of their development. Casework goals were considered to be: (1) helping clients to change; or (2) to maintain themselves at an adequate level of functioning.

REFERENCES

Books

Robinson, Virginia: *A Changing Psychology in Social Casework*. North Carolina, University of North Carolina Press, 1939.

Pamphlets

Differential Approach in Casework Treatment. New York, Family Welfare Association of America, 1936, pp. 1-64.

Articles

Aspects of relations with the community in family case work, *The Family, XX:* 2:35-49, April 1939.

Aspects of relations with the community in family case work. Part II, *The Family, XX:* 3:80-86, May 1939.

A study of 229 cases referred to family casework agencies by the Court of Domestic Relations of Brooklyn, *The Family, XVII:* 3:81-85, May 1936.

Austin, Lucille Nickel: The evolution of our social case work concepts, *The Family, XX:* 3:42-47, April 1939.

Boggs, Marjorie: Family social work in relation to family life, *The Family, XV:* 5:146-152, July 1934.

———————— and Eastman, Helen: Services available in a private family agency, *The Family, XV:* 10:334-337, February 1935.

Cannon, Antoinette: Where the changes in social casework have brought us, *The Family, XV:* 9:224-244, January 1935.

Day, Florence R.: Changing practices in casework treatment, *The Family, XVIII:* 1:3-10, March 1937.

Deihl, Nannie E., and Wilson, Robert S.: Can listening become a casework art? *The Family, XIV:* 4:99-105, June 1933.

Eaves, Lucile: Studies of breakdowns in family income, *The Family, X:* 8:227-232, December 1929.

Fitch, John A.: The responsibility of social work in an economic crisis, *The Family, XII:* 2:50-54, April 1931.

Garrett, Annette: Case work teaching by the casework method, *The Family, XX:* 7:211-216, November 1939.

Gartland, Ruth: The child, the parent and the agency, *The Family, XVIII:* 3:75-80, March 1937.

Hamilton, Gordon: Basic concepts in social casework, *The Family*, *XVIII:* 5:147-156, July 1937.

————————: Refocusing family casework, *The Family, XII:* 6:174-183, October 1931.

Hollis, Florence: Individualized service to families in the private agency, *The Family, XIX:* 6:181-187, October 1938.

————————. The function of a family society, *The Family, XII:* 6:186-191, October 1931.

Kahn, Dorothy C.: Experiment in selective intake in a family society, *The Family, XIII:* 1:3-8, March 1932.

Kasius, Cora. Some questions of family agency program in relation to interpretation, *The Family, XVII:* 3:67-71, May 1936.

Lee, Porter R.: Social case work, *The Family, XV:* 7:199-204, November 1934.

Lowry, Fern: Casework skills and fundamental human needs, *The Family, XIV:* 5:159-163, July 1933.

————————: Objectives in social casework, *The Family, XVIII:* 8:263-268, December 1937.

Marcus, Grace F.: Psychological realities and casework, *The Family, XIII:* 5:147-150, July 1932.

————————: Some implications for casework of Rank's psychology, *The Family, XVIII:* 8:272-277, December 1937.

————————: Some tentative methods of adjusting case load, *The Family, XI:* 6:182-189, October 1930.

McLean, Francis: Present day problems in the family field, *The Family, XII:* 6:170-173, October 1931.

————————: The casework laboratory, *The Family, XV:* 2:54-57, April 1934.

————————: The casework laboratory, *The Family, XV:* 3:90-92, May 1934.

Merrill, Laura A.: The caseworker's role in treatment, *The Family, XIII:* 5:156-158, July 1932.

Millar, Margaret: Common and specialized services in family and children's agencies, *The Family, XX:* 7:222-228, November 1939.

Mowrer, Harriet R.: Domestic discord, personality adjustment, and the court, *The Family, XV:* 4:103-109, May 1934.

Neustaedter, Eleanor: Along what lines does the future contribution of the family welfare movement lie? *The Family, XX:* 4:123-129, June 1939.

------------: The role of the caseworker in treatment, *The Family*, *XIII:* 5:151-156, July 1932.

------------: The social caseworker and industrial depression, *The Family*, *XI:* 9:275-279, January 1931.

Ogburn, William F.: The changing family, *The Family*, *XIX:* 5:139-143, July 1938.

Ramsdell, Leroy: Some ideals to guide practical administration of unemployment relief, *The Family*, *XIII:* 10:323-327, February, 1933.

Raymond, Stockton: The family society today, *The Family*, *XIV:* 2:46-50, April 1933.

Reed, Ellery F.: The classification of case work problems, *The Family*, *VI:* 3:83-85, May 1930.

Reynolds, Bertha C.: A changing psychology in social casework, *The Family*, *XII:* 4:99-112, June 1931.

------------: A changing psychology in social casework, after one year, *The Family*, *XIII:* 4:107-111, June 1932.

------------: Social casework, what is it? What is its place in the world today? *The Family*, *XVI:* 8:235-242, December 1935.

------------: They have neither money nor work, *The Family*, *XII:* 2:35-39, April 1931.

Rich, Margaret E.: Family social work and family life, *The Family*, *XV:* 5:152-156, July 1934.

------------: The caseworker in action, *The Family*, *XI:* 4:117-123, June 1930.

------------: The philosophy and program of a private family agency, *The Family*, *XIX:* 9:283-289, January 1939.

Sanderson, John P.: The family society of tomorrow, *The Family*, *XIV:* 2:41-43, April 1933.

Stapleford, F. N.: Some challenges to private family social work, *The Family*, *XVI:* 7:197-201, November 1935.

Starr, Josephine S.: How can the family agencies be better prepared for the next economic depression? *The Family*, *XII:* 9, 274-279, January 1932.

Swift, Linton B.: The purpose and program of a family case work agency, *The Family*, *XX:* 1:3-7, March 1939.

------------: The relief problem in family social work, *The Family*, *X:* 1:3-11, March 1929.

Waite, Florence T.: A little matter of self-respect, *The Family*, *XVII:* 1:12-13, March 1936.

Wallerstein, Helen: New trends in casework as developed by the depression, *The Family*, *XV:* 7:206-210, November 1934.

Ware, Anna Budd: Family agencies' responsibility and practice during an unemployment period, *The Family*, *XII:* 10:302-306, February 1932.

White, Helen C.: Activity in the casework relationship, *The Family*, *XIV:* 6:203-208, October 1933.

White, Helen V.: Casework challenged, *The Family*, *XII:* 2:60-62, April 1931.

White, R. Clyde: The relative value of case study and statistics, *The Family*, *X:* 9:259-265, January 1930.

Chapter IV

WORLD WAR II, DECADE 1940-1949

The greatest paradox of them all is still civilized warfare.
SOURCE UNKNOWN

SOCIAL CHANGE

WAR AND THE FAMILY: During this period, which includes the years of World War II, the emphasis was on a program of family casework service to troubled individuals and unhappy families in an attempt to help them lead more satisfying lives so that they could make an adequate contribution to their community.

War meant unnatural separations between parents and sons, wives and husbands, fathers and young children. There were separations of family members brought about by a concentration of job opportunities in certain cities and localities. Caseworkers grew concerned over the rapidly developing trend for women to work outside the home when their presence was considered to be essential to the preservation of family values. As mothers went to work, marital problems became increasingly complex and the difficulties tended to continue over long periods of time.

Foster day care for children of working mothers was not readily solved. Eventually day nurseries were established to care for the children of employed mothers. When both parents were absent from the home, juvenile delinquency appeared to increase among the adolescent age group. Young girls had troubles caused by love affairs with soldiers. Problems of mother-son relationships became more apparent and there was an increase in unmarried mothers. Young girls who had been married only a few months and who were attempting to continue their former way of life while their husbands were away encountered problems in their wartime marriages. To some it seemed that the family was being "torn asunder."

Inadequate housing presented problems in defense communities and many cities developed trailer slums. Problems of the times for which clients sought help included:

a) Decisions in choice of expenditure of income.
b) Working out debt adjustments.
c) Help in setting up a home apart from the parents of married couples.
d) Decisions regarding problems of change of employment.
e) Whether to remain in school or seek employment.
f) Difficulties resulting from husband and wife separations.
g) Help in re-establishing or maintaining broken homes.
h) Troubles involved in the placement and finding of foster homes for children.

Toward the end of this decade, there were problems in the area of the adjustment of returning soldiers to civilian life. Those men who had adapted too well to the subordinate role required by military life had difficulty regaining those strengths necessary for success in the competitive individualistic form of civilian life. As civilians they needed to begin again to make decisions without recourse to authority. Conversely, "decision-makers" such as commissioned or non-commissioned military personnel, often experienced difficulties fitting into subordinate positions.

THE FAMILY

SOCIAL CHANGE AND THE FAMILY: During the thirties, family morale had been lowered by unemployment and families were held together through necessity. Total defense for war now meant military and industrial mobilization. Great new arms factories sprang up overnight on the outskirts of once leisurely cities. Men and women were recruited from all over the country to operate these factories. This resulted in the migration of thousands from their home localities to these new areas of employment. However, the problems of unemployment were still in evidence as entire industries of great size were closed by government order. Closing the doors of established industries meant an additional shift in the labor market with the accompanying family uncertainties and loss of the family standard of living. For the employed, industry was no longer a paternalistic organization where the faithful employee was protected. Industry was now succumbing to the impersonal, ruthless pressures attendant to large-scale production and was requiring greater occupational skill of its employees.

Those with German, Italian or Japanese ancestry were considered aliens and enemies to the security of the nation. They were often discharged from industry and public employment and their internment was a widespread practice. Dislocated families who had no legal residence were in dire need. Working with families with racial and cultural differences meant recognizing and understanding differences.

The influence of such social inventions as apartments, day nurseries, and the factory system all combined to reduce further the economic functions of the family. There was rapid dissemination of information, especially through use of the radio. The family searched for entertainment outside the home and patronized movies and summer camps for children. All these changes influenced the family in a variety of ways.

A typical American family consisted of a husband and wife and one or more children. Often they were living in a community where they did not know anyone, where they had no relatives and had to depend upon a "sitter" for care of the children. In the past it had been the father who was the disciplinarian of the children. This responsibility was increasingly being turned over to the mother. The father was now doing more in a material way for the children than he had ever done before.

Recognition of hostility and aggression in the family had long been contrary to the still influential puritanical ideals, but these elements were known to exist in every family. The client and caseworker now were facing this uncontrolled hostility within a family, recognizing it as such, and working with it. The clients' uncontrolled "acting out" and their physiological symptoms were considered to be two different expressions of disturbed intra-family relationships. The family was seen as the medium in which these intense disturbed interpersonal relationships could be worked out rather than turned inward through repression, into crippling symptoms.

The attitudes toward sex discussion were changing and there was a freer communication about sex problems. The former prudish suppression which had led to anxiety and emotional disturbances now gave way to forthright inquiry and uninhibited discussion of sex problems.

Social change brought about a change in the institutional roles of the family of the past to what was now being referred to as "companionship relations." This meant that individualism was replacing traditional familism. The principle of equality as applied to each member of the family structure was replacing the one-time authoritarian control of the family by the father. The family still, however, provided its members with a sense of emotional security through mutual love, altruism and self-sacrifice. The important remaining functions of the family were the satisfaction of the needs for intimate affectional response, of socialization, personality patterning, and reproduction.

Much, if not most, of the pathology noted in the modern family of the forties was seen by many authorities as related to change in *family patterns* which in turn was traceable to changes in the industrial society. What had been viewed as family disintegration could well be studied as a phase of the social reorientation of the family in adjusting to a deep and far-reaching recasting of the total family. With the shift in family control from one of authoritarian domination to one of greater equalitarianism, love between family members increased in importance as a factor in family stability.

During this period, a large number of social workers went into industrial settings as well as day nurseries, relocation centers, army rehabilitation camps and schools. As caseworkers in private agencies were relieved of certain areas of casework, they turned their attention to casework service for families in the long-time chronic need group.

THE CASEWORKER

CHRONIC CASES: For many years it had been known that there were responses, both positive and negative, between clients and caseworkers and that treatment was facilitated or hindered by intangibles in these responses. Caseworkers attempted to examine the total dynamic situation of acting and being acted upon. As one writer stated: "Sometimes by dealing with him [the client] in such an isolated fashion, we have fallen in with his own pattern of needing to have everything, including the caseworker, for himself."[1] Cases not responding to treatment were closely and critically scrutinized in an effort to determine the reasons for lack of movement. Casework efforts were spread with a mechanical evenness over both "hopeful" and "less hopeful" cases. The question of the day was, "Just how effective is casework with extreme and chronic cases?" Opinions on this question were divided. Some believed it would be well to be more discriminating in the use of casework skills. They felt that the client with a limited capacity for growth presented a discouraging problem; therefore, they questioned the justification of caseworkers spending a considerable amount of time and effort with chronic cases when so many others seemingly could utilize casework services more profitably. Frank Bruno suggested that the more hopeless cases be given just enough attention to insure freedom from neglect thus allowing caseworkers to concentrate on the more hopeful cases which could be brought to a successful outcome.[2]

Caseworkers were also critically examining their tendency to overlook clients who were not readily seeking casework help. This was particularly true in relation to psychopaths who did not seem to feel the need for help in "a better use of self." The opinion held was that they were best helped not by financial assistance but by a firm, though understanding, insistence that they meet their responsibilities.

MEANING OF MONEY: The government's acceptance of responsibility for relief giving during the last decade did more than sharpen the distinction between public and private agencies. It increased the variation between administration of relief and the

---

[1] Florence T. Waite: Case work—today and fifty years ago, *The Family*, XXI, February, 1941, p. 322.

[2] Frank J. Bruno: Guide, philosopher, and friend, *Journal of Social Casework*, XXVII, March, 1946, p. 12.

diagnosis of social pathology. Caseworkers in private agencies were giving more services to families who needed only a small amount of financial assistance for a limited period of time. Workers were no longer so concerned with whether or not the client was "entitled" to relief but were more interested in the nature of the client's needs. They believed that attention should be directed to caseworker-client participation in the helping process within the scope and limitations of the client's capacity to use the service and the caseworker's skill in giving the service. With the rising cost of living came a renewed interest in making available to the families data and services from the fields of home economics and nutrition. However, when the client's financial needs were greater than the agency could meet, caseworkers often overlooked discussing the client's budgetary problems largely because of their own anxiety.

In this decade, Annette Garrett commented that caseworkers had felt "everything would be all right" if people only had enough money. On the basis of the sound relief practices developed by welfare services during the thirties, caseworkers were now more than ever before acknowledging the need for proper handling of the emotional factors involved in both the giving and receiving of relief.[1] As Herbert Aptekar expressed it, "Relief produces little relief, . . . relief solved problems, but in so doing, also created problems."[2] Relief giving and relief receiving were not considered peaceful pursuits because of the conflict involved as a result of the imposed obligations and responsibility in the mind of both the giver and the receiver. When these obligations and responsibilities came between client and caseworker, it was necessary to detect and correct the negative effects.

Caseworkers were examining the objective and symbolic meanings of money as a source and locus of power. Because the money might be used to show acceptance of a client, or to get acceptance from him, to show authority or lack of authority, or to be an indulgent parent or a punishing one, the ability to give or withhold

---

1 Annette Garrett: The professional base of social casework, *Journal of Social Casework*, XXVII, July, 1946, p. 167.

2 Herbert H. Aptekar: Principles of relief giving in a family agency, *The Family*, XXI, October, 1940, p. 194.

money was seen as having deep emotional implications for the caseworker. Caseworkers, therefore, felt they needed to understand their own feelings toward money and the unmet financial needs in the community in order to prevent their own needs and bias from interfering with accurate diagnostic evaluation or treatment skills.

The client's requests for financial assistance were categorized as: (1) Requests expressed in terms of money, but where the actual need was something quite different. (2) Requests by those who had been able to work out their adjustments, but for whom some crisis had occurred that created a temporary financial need. (3) Requests by persons who had sufficient income but who for a variety of reasons had some temporary or intermittent financial need.[1]

The giving of financial assistance was used as an aid in exploring new and unmet areas of the clients' needs. This was a significant change from the relief giving practices of the past. Casework services were extended to the marginal income and economically independent families. Private agencies initiated fee charging for their casework services. *Relief giving was used as tool in treatment directed toward the goal of fostering the development of wholesome family life through assisting individuals to lead satisfying and socially useful lives.*

FAMILY CENTERED CASEWORK: Caseworkers exhibited greater awareness of the strains, jealousies, and antagonisms found among members of the family and increasingly extended their services to more than one member of the family. They found casework services might be refused by some members of the family, that help might not be wanted for all their problems, and that clients varied in the kind and amount of help they desired and needed. The unique contribution of the caseworker in the solution of family and marriage problems was his ability to see the individual in relation to his total setting and then draw on his general knowledge in the field of family relations as an aid in giving casework services.[2]

---

1 Dorothy V. Thomas: Criteria for the giving of financial assistance in a private family agency, *Journal of Social Casework*, XXVIII, May, 1947, p. 183.

2 Margaret E. Rich: A modern spirit in casework, *Journal of Social Casework*, XXVII, March, 1946, p. 20.

MARRIAGE COUNSELING: A more active and direct approach to the client was used in counseling for marital problems. This was done to test the client's desire and capacity to work on the problem. Caseworkers often found that the clients in marriage counseling were their educational equals. The specific techniques of casework applicable to marriage problems were the basic principles of differential diagnosis and treatment. At this time Frances McLean identified seven aspects of family life as: the environment, the mental, physical and moral condition of the different family members, their industrial efficiency, their temperamental traits, and the family solidarity.[1] Clients sought help because they were concerned about their relationship with their spouse, and because they were anxious, tense and in conflict. It was discovered that changes in the client invariably produced problems for those closest to him. Therefore, the caseworker emphasized the need to involve both members of the marriage thus enabling each one to anticipate and deal with his reactions to the changed behavior of the other family member.

Because of the many changes occurring within the family there was an increased emphasis placed on family counseling and family education. A continued analysis was made of new types of crises which interfered with marital adjustment as these developed.

Psychological problems of marital adjustment often included financial needs as well as help with problems such as the family budget, child care, household management, and health and nursing problems. This required that the caseworker have an understanding of the individual and be sufficiently able to evaluate which situations were acute and which were chronic. The worker would then be in a position to choose the treatment accordingly.

Mabel Rasey stated that clients seeking marriage counseling could be divided into three groups: (1) Those clients needing straight counseling; that is, those cases that dealt with the client's inner pressures of anxiety and confusion resulting from the attitudes of either or both partners: (2) those cases that primarily

---

[1] *Ibid.*

needed environmental aid, and (3) a combination of the first two groups, those who needed both counseling and relief.[1]

Due to the war, there was an impetus of pressure, haste, urgency, mobility and action. Problems of marital discord were often the result of separation with no time for reconciliation. In haste, parents were placing children in homes of their own choice. Caseworkers felt it was easy to be trapped into accepting the urgency of quick decisions, thus resulting in casework which was not meeting the needs of the client. When this occurred, neither the client nor the caseworker was satisfied with the services being given. Florence Day noted that caseworker skills needed to be quickened and sharpened, based on the observation that the reality of the day demanded reorientation to an almost complete reversal of circumstances.

> It seems just yesterday that reality appeared in the shape of morale lowered by unemployment, hopes and plans stymied by curtailed income, childhood dependency prolonged through lack of opportunity to assume adult responsibilities, families held together involuntarily, hampered from freedom of individual movement . . . [Today] War is a major disaster which affects the lives of all of us to a greater or less degree. Individuals and families bear the brunt as the usual emotional and social equilibrium is upset and dislocations are imposed on the familiar way of life.[2]

In the forties, caseworkers felt that they did not have sufficient time to examine the total family picture and the forces within it that created or increased problems. They needed to direct their efforts to securing significant material with greater rapidity and accuracy.

The increasing emphasis on the rights of the individual and decreasing emphasis on his responsibilities as a member of the family

---

[1] Mabel Rasey: Marriage counseling in a family agency, *The Family*, XXIV, April, 1943, p. 65.

[2] Florence Day: Sharpening methods to meet present needs, *The Family*, XXIV, February, 1944, p. 363.

and as a member of society seemed to lead caseworkers to think too exclusively of the rights desired by a single member.

PROFESSIONAL VOCABULARY: There was a continued effort to cope with the problem of establishing a standard professional vocabulary. There appeared to be no solution to the problem of semantics. As Jeanette Regenburg wrote, "The words, principles, philosophy, concepts, methods, and process have from time to time been used as practically synonymous."[1]

CASEWORK

General Methods

THE FUNCTIONAL SCHOOL: The decade of the forties produced the functional and diagnostic schools of thought. The general methods of both schools were developed and continued to grow in recognition.

The basic psychology of the functional school of thought is traceable to Otto Rank's "will" psychology with its focus on the "ego" or self.[2] This school stressed that the source of healing and helping power was part of the individual's innate power to grow, to change, and to use selectively experience not only to his own ends but to the exercise of his own will. The functionalists believed the problem for which the client sought help to be centered around the client's relationship to his *situation.* The client was to be helped in such a manner as to support and stimulate him to use all his available capacities for decision and action in relation to that *particular problem* in his situation. The fundamental dynamic was the emphasis placed on the social agency as represented by the caseworker in the social casework helping process. This was the most characteristic differentiating factor from the diagnostic school.

Through the agency function and the control of the process of interaction between worker and client, the connections are

---

[1] Jeanette Regenburg: Classroom instruction in social casework, *The Family,* XXI, June, 1940, p. 117.

[2] Grace F. Marcus: Family casework in 1948, *Journal of Social Casework,* XXIX, July, 1948, p. 251.

made between the unfolding, changing problem, the developing decisions of the client for dealing with it within the bonds
of the agency's service, and the developing consequences . . .
The emphasis on functional limits stands in sharp contrast to
the broadly receptive policy of the agency using the diagnostic
approach.[1]

The functional approach was a "helping process in the offering of
a service whose use and whose outcome is under the control of
the recipient of help, not of the professional worker."[2]

It was through the agency's definition and limitation of function
and policy that the client was offered a new experience in yield-
ing himself to a fixed social reality while retaining his own integrity. The interviews were considered to be a "genuine experiencing" for the client. The caseworker knew only those parts of the
life and actions of the client that the *client revealed in the interview.* "They [The functional school] stressed limits of time, beginning, ending, separation, and considered particularly that part of
the person which is 'well enough to use help.' "[3] This was not considered to be the same as knowing *about* the client. The outcome
of casework was not considered to be predictable as it was the
client who made the decision. The functionalists rejected Mary
Richmond's concept of social diagnosis.

THE DIAGNOSTIC SCHOOL: Social diagnosis consisted of a systematic effort to identify relevant psycho-social data, evaluate its
significance and appraise the possibility of change and improvement in the client.[4]

Much of the theoretical framework of the diagnostic school of
thought was derived from Freudian psychoanalysis. Grace Marcus, in an attempt to point out the differences between the two

---

[1] *Ibid.,* p. 263-269.

[2] Kenneth L. M. Pray: A restatement of the generic principles of social casework practice, *Journal of Social Casework,* XXVIII, October, 1947, p. 258.

[3] Gordon Hamilton: The underlying philosophy of social case work, *The Family,* XXII,
July, 1941, p. 143.

[4] Patricia Sacks: Establishing the diagnosis in marital problems, *Journal of Social Casework,* XXX, May, 1949, p. 183.

schools, summed up the diagnostic treatment approach as, (1) involving the nature of the problem; (2) the psychodynamics of the case; (3) the actual life circumstances of the client; (4) the worker's capacities; (5) the agency function, and (6) community resources available to help the client differentially in the light of all those varying factors.[1] This meant being aware of the client as a person as he reacted to his social reality and to those in close relationship to him. The client was seen as one who was acted upon by other personalities and sets of circumstances which were beyond his immediate control. He was envisioned as an individual who fashioned reality to suit his own needs. Social diagnosis focused on the client's total dynamic situation of acting and being acted upon and also involved an appraisal of each client's behavior and personality in terms of his current capacities in relation to his past experiences.

In arriving at a diagnostic formulation, it was essential for the caseworker to consider (a) the total psychic structure of the person; (b) nature and degree of his symptomology; (c) the caliber of his intellect and judgment; (d) the social desirability of his behavior, and (e) the effectiveness and appropriateness of his adaptive mechanisms. The tensions produced from within the individual and the tensions and pressures proceeding from difficulties arising outside the person were used as a basis for social diagnosis, and called for a wide range of treatment methods.

The casework methods of the diagnostic school provided supportive or insight therapy. The *supportive method* helped clients maintain their present capacities for functioning. *Insight therapy* helped those clients who were capable of growth in their conscious understanding and control of themselves. The transference relationship was used to help clients eventually take independent command of their life situations. The casework focus was more on problems within the individual.[2] The diagnostic school attempted to determine results in casework.

Gordon Hamilton summarized the disagreement between the two schools of thought by stating that the diagnostic group placed

[1] Marcus: *loc. cit.*

[2] Marcus: *loc. cit.*

emphasis on the diagnostic element with "need" as the basis of practice and agency function considered a necessary division of labor. However, the functionalists considered agency function the basis of practice with a primary focus on evaluation of the client's purpose in a particular situation.[1]

HOMEOSTASIS: In medical terminology, homeostasis is often referred to as "the organism's efforts toward maintenance of ease." Eleanor Cockerill pointed out that sometimes disequilibrium caused by a social situation was as important to consider as a person's physical adaptation. She referred to the state of disequilibrium as "lack of ease" of the organism in adjustment, but stated that: "We have, no doubt, acquired even greater respect for the adaptive mechanism with which the human being is endowed."[2]

Maintaining the organism's physio-psycho-sociological balance was considered to be the chief function of the ego and was referred to as homeostasis. The caseworker used this principle as an aid to gain an understanding of the client's behavior and his use of defense mechanisms which he employed in an attempt to maintain his equilibrium.

PSYCHO-SOCIAL CASEWORK: In 1949, Florence Hollis referred to all casework as "psycho-social." She pointed out that internal and external problems were present in causation and treatment, but that the psychological and social components would vary in importance. In psycho-social diagnosis, four levels of treatment were identified: (1) modifying the environment; (2) psychological support; (3) clarification (sometimes called counseling) — support and clarification usually went hand in hand, and (4) insight. The insight method of casework treatment was considered deeper treatment than gained through clarification. Insight was defined as the process of relieving the client's current and past emotions in a therapeutic atmosphere. This emotional release was encouraged in order to discharge the client's affect thus bringing irrationalities to the surface. This release allowed the client to recognize these

---

1 Gordon Hamilton: *op. cit.,* p. 139-147.

2 Eleanor Cockerill: New emphasis on an old concept in medicine, *Journal of Social Casework,* XXX, January, 1949, p. 11.

irrationalities, at first in the safety of the treatment situation and later in life situations.[1]

Procedure and Techniques

THE INTERVIEW: *The primary casework technique was the interview, the initial intake interview and the succeeding interviews.* Miss Garrett quoted Dr. Levy[2] as stating that the most valuable contribution of psychoanalysis was the increased knowledge of the importance of providing a non-judgmental, sympathetic audience for the client within the office interview and with regular appointments at definite periods of time.[3]

In both the initial interview and succeeding ones, the caseworker, by virtue of training and sensitivity, was expected to communicate to the troubled person a feeling of being "with" him. This was seen as "professional identification," through which the caseworker accepted the fact that the client had a problem and expressed interest in helping the client continue to define and do something about this problem.

Six social casework interviewing procedures were specifically differentiated in 1940:

(1) There must be recognition of any person's right to his own feelings, opinions, wishes, standards of behavior. (2) The client's internal balance must be maintained. (3) The caseworker needs to maintain a professional relationship with the client. (4) The worker recognizes and acts upon the client's right to understand what is being done, as well as agreeing to it. (5) Do not judge or act until the situation is understood from the client's point of view, no matter what the relation may be to objective reality. (6) If there was interpretation of feeling, or behavior, or a suggested plan of treatment, case-

---

[1] Florence Hollis: The techniques of casework, *Journal of Social Casework*, XXX, June, 1949, p. 235-244.

[2] David M. Levy, M.D. (1892-   ), was Chief of Staff, New York Institute for Child Guidance, 1927-1933.

[3] Annette Garrett: Transference in casework, *The Family*, XXII, April, 1941, p. 44.

workers were systematically challenging themselves to make it possible for the client to explain, reject, or accept.[1]

Casework techniques used within the interview were listening, direct teaching, and indirect teaching through discussion and activity. Interviewing techniques required skill in the ability to help people to talk, in establishing a positive relationship, in obtaining information, in noting clues that revealed more fundamental problems underlying the client's verbalized ones, and skill in fitting treatment procedures appropriately to the needs of the individual client. Because of the caseworker's lack of skill in understanding and management of the transference in the client-caseworker relationship, maximum use was not always made of these techniques.

INTAKE INTERVIEW: The direction of the initial interview was what differentiated the intake interview and continuing interviews. The main responsibility of the caseworker in the initial interview was to help clients feel less insecure and anxious so that they could express themselves more freely. The initial interview was used to allow the client to explain his difficulty, what it seemed to mean to him, how he felt about it and what he felt should be done. The caseworker endeavored to enter each casework relationship with a certain outgoing receptive frame of mind that would enable clients to feel they were understood and respected. If there were anxiety and insecurity on the part of the caseworker to such a point that it interfered with the client's need to talk about his situation, it was believed that the opportunity to help the client might be lost. The caseworker needed to understand and accept the client's anxiety in facing his problems and appreciate his difficulty in having to ask for help. This relationship was necessary for often the manner in which a client expressed his needs indicated the type of person he was and why he was faced with this particular situation.

When caseworkers gave their attention to the client's problem, even though unverbalized, the client felt the interest, sincerity, sympathy, understanding, objectivity, and tolerance of the caseworker. The core of the initial interview encompassed a process

---

1 Regenburg: op. cit., p. 118.

whereby the client and caseworker together would explore the client's difficulty. It was hoped this would permit a tentative diagnosis which would indicate further steps and procedure. The concluding portion of the first interview was directed toward bringing the presented problem into final focus. The client-worker relationship would then be used in further interviews to help the client to deal with what he would discover to be the *real* problem.

THE RELATIONSHIP: Virginia Robinson, in her book *A Changing Psychology in Social Casework,* delineated the many-sided meanings of the client-caseworker relationship. She emphasized that the one common quality underlying the attitudes of clients seeking casework help was the active search for a "relationship" in which to solve a problem.[1] Closely related to this process was the question, "What use would the client make of the caseworker?"[2] Thus, casework diagnosis involved an understanding of the client's social situation, the psychological aspects and the specific tangible service he was requesting, and an analysis of what use the client would attempt to make of casework services.

In 1943, Robert Gomberg specifically spelled out use of the client-caseworker relationship as being directed to the client's "more satisfying use of self." He believed that in the security of this relationship, the client's social reality situation was easily observable, specifically the standard of living, job status, family composition, or conformity to social mores. The client's psychological reality was less recognizable because this reality was essentially dominated by feeling. The client might be in control of his feelings or might be deeply disturbed, anxious, discouraged, or hostile out of proportion. It was the degree of balance that an individual maintained between his social and psychological reality which indicated his degree of integration of self and the stability of his personality, as well as the amount of his functioning capacity.

As the caseworker gained an understanding of the ego functioning of the client, he was able to utilize this in the helping proc-

---

[1] Florence Sytz: The unit of attention in the casework process, *Journal of Social Casework,* XXVII, June, 1946, p. 136.

[2] *Ibid.*

ess to give direction to the activity of the client. Over the course of the contacts and with the help of the casework relationship, the client was helped to give up slowly erratic behavior and to begin to integrate his activities. It was anticipated that the client would eventually begin to assimilate the constructive ego and a more constructive use of self; and that he would transfer, gradually, this use of self to activity outside the casework relationship.[1]

CLIENT PARTICIPATION: It was now considered a truism that an individual could be helped only with those needs he recognized and for which he wished help. Thus, the client was given the responsibility of defining his need as he saw it and requesting the services he felt would meet his need. The client was encouraged to express his own need; and when the client had identified a problem or "sore spot," attempts by the caseworker to divert the client or ignore this problem generally resulted in the client's not returning.

Casework was not principally predicated on changing the individual but on giving him the time and opportunity to understand and see his own problem and the possible adjustment he could make. Many casework failures were considered to be attributable to the caseworker's inability to see the client's point of view. The primary test in the casework situation was a clarification of what the client was seeking to satisfy and how he was interfering with such satisfaction. "You beat your wife. You don't want to beat your wife. Why do you beat your wife?" It was not a question of the caseworker's *allowing* the client to participate but it was believed the client *must* do so if the experience was to be a dynamic and meaningful one for him.

SELF-DETERMINATION: Increased recognition was being given to the belief that the worth and importance of the individual in being self-determining must be consistent along with his capacity to be self-determining. Helping the client to think through his problems and to make decisions was of primary importance, yet the caseworker needed to refrain from verbally stating that no one else could make his decisions for him as such a statement could

---

[1] M. Robert Gomberg: Function as a psychological concept in casework theory, *The Family*, XXIV, April, 1943, p. 56.

block the client's request for help. The caseworker's attitude was expected to be non-judgmental, objective and used as an aid in releasing the client's capacities for self-direction and as an opportunity to shape his own future effectiveness in living.

SHORT-TERM CASES: Considerable attention was focused on short-term contacts during the forties. Skill in short contact interviewing was a necessity as requests from working mothers who wished to place their children increased. One of the critical questions asked was whether or not caseworkers should encourage mothers to work. Some mothers needed help in seeing that their greatest contribution was in the home, meeting the needs of their own families. Many mothers who were seeking help focused their discussion on financial need as the sole basis for their employment and discussed *only* the most superficial aspects of plans for care of the child.

Another question posed in regard to short-term cases was: "How could the caseworker carry out the delicate task of helping the client see the pros and cons of the problem realistically yet still leave the client free to make his own decisions?" The role of the caseworker was a difficult one because of the importance of a good working relationship, the need to handle constructively the urgency of the situation and at the same time arrive at an adequate diagnosis.

Treatment Goals

GOAL-CENTERED TREATMENT: *Casework during the forties was more goal-centered. The goal in treatment pre-supposed sufficient diagnostic understanding to select some specific area that might be the kernel of the client's problem.*

Treatment was considered to begin with the initial client-caseworker contact. The first step was a mutual understanding of the situation as it existed in the present. The second step was the caseworker's efforts to understand the causative factors, and the third step was the establishment of a plan which would enable the caseworker and client to work together toward improving the situation. Rather than have no goal at all, it was believed better to delimit certain areas for discussion with the client and be ready to shift the goals and area if indicated.[1] It was found that mistakes had been made in the past, when it was thought to be better to have no goal but to "wander on" hoping that if everything was included, everything would eventually be solved.

Dr. Levy is quoted as stating that the caseworker should have three casework goals: (1) a tentative diagnosis of the unconscious factors in the client: (2) delimitation of the treatment goal in the formulation of a tentative treatment plan, and (3) understanding and management of the transference.[2]

Social Diagnosis, pointed out one writer, is not a mere label or categorical diagnosis, rather it should be a statement clearly delineating the type of person, his general make-up and methods of functioning, his deviations from accepted normal behavior and the probable reasons for the deviations. The objective was to forecast the course, the duration and the outcome of the client's maladjustment, in the light of the casework treatment. It was deemed important that the casework treatment plan reveal the choice of procedure, and the aims or goals of treatment. The plan of treatment for the client needed to clarify whether: (a) complete rehabilitation was proposed with total relief of the client's problem; (b) partial readjustment and solution of the problem; or (c) an attempt to help the client adjust as he was, without intrinsic change, but through new or modified environment or social situation.[3]

The provision of a framework by the division of casework into investigation, diagnosis, and treatment in the past decades was an effort to define manageable parts. However, this did not end attempts to find units of the three steps that were more compassable to further insight and control. Now, the purpose of the "investigation" was "seeking ways of helpfulness" was "a creative search for the possibilities of people."[4] It was the opinion of Florence

---

[1] Garrett: Transference in casework, p. 42.

[2] Garrett: *Ibid*.

[3] LeRoy Meader: Diagnostic criteria—The concept of normal and abnormal, *The Family*, XXII, October, 1941, p. 141.

[4] Rich: *op. cit.*, p. 20.

Sytz that the investigation in casework was still tending to be stronger than the treatment and that a more penetrating helpful action was needed than was currently being given. "Caseworkers as well as clients are not immune from the temptation to take the probable location of a difficulty for its solution, although the functional aspects of the problem remain to be solved."[1]

Although it was possible to think of social study and treatment as the casework process, the parts that made up the process still needed to be broken down further into manageable sections in order for the techniques and procedures of the caseworker to be outlined definitively. *Skill in casework was now considered to be the discerning and developing of the clients' inherent strengths, not the patching up of weaknesses.*

In 1949, casework was defined in terms of three specific objectives. They were: (1) giving help to clients with environmental problems; (2) supportive therapy, and (3) intermediate and insight therapy.

Environmental problems were those requiring help with practical tangible problems.

Supportive therapy was referred to as evaluation of the client's social situation, capacities and limitations. The goal of ego supportive therapy was to help maintain the client's present adjustment, and to maintain existing strengths, with little re-integration of the personality expected. Cases where use of supportive therapy was indicated were the alcoholic, pre-and post-psychotic and psychopathic personalities.

The third objective, intermediary and insight therapy, meant that the casework emphasis was directed toward "personal factors" and to the interaction in the caseworker-client relationship. The shifts in feeling within the interview, and in the course of treatment, and reactions to past experiences were more heavily weighted than in the social environment and supportive cases. The aim in treatment was to help the individual change old patterns of behavior: "to attain a more satisfactory use of himself."[2]

---

[1] Sytz: *op. sit.*, p. 136.

[2] Ruby Little: Diagnostic recording, *Journal of Social Casework*, XXX, January, 1949, p. 18.

In general, casework treatment goals were directed toward helping clients live socially useful lives. A socially useful life was defined as a life that would give as well as take, that would acknowledge the rights of others while asserting its own, a life that accepted duties and responsibilities as well as privileges and immunities.[1]

MARRIAGE COUNSELING TREATMENT TRENDS: Marital problems usually called for a quick working diagnosis supported by appropriate treatment. Locating both the personality factors causing the difficulty and the corresponding strengths which would be utilized in working with the client was of the utmost importance. The continued evaluation and alertness to the client's progress, his "back-sliding" or his immobility were seen as an important requisite throughout the counseling process. Continued experience in marriage counseling and evaluation of casework now revealed that successful treatment involved approximately three steps: (1) defining the problem and accepting it with the client; (2) the examination of the conscious or nearly conscious causes underlying the difficulty, thus creating awareness of the correction needed or the goal to be desired; and finally (3) the help the caseworker would give the client in the actual re-education or retraining process.

CHRONIC CASES: In chronic need groups, goals were being more clearly defined by discriminating between external and emotional factors, thus enabling clearer evaluations of strengths and limitations of clients and a clearer definition of the areas in which caseworkers could be of help. Obtaining relief from public welfare had not answered the chronic need group's problems and the problem of how to provide successful casework services with this group had not been solved. Chronic cases were still labeled: "untreatable," "uncooperative," or "hopeless."

UTILIZATION OF THE CASE RECORD: The use of case recordings was an invaluable aid in defining treatment objectives. A case record included the caseworker's social study and diagnostic statement and stated the client's problem and the nature of the client's request. The case record was also expected to include relevant

---

1 Waite: *loc. cit.*

social data and pertinent emotional material, the movement or progress to date, and finally a diagnostic statement with a plan of treatment. Social diagnosis was always considered fluid—that is, subject to change and correction due to additional information that might come to light or due to modification induced by treatment. The basis for measurement of casework treatment was the client's growth.

SUMMARY OF THE 1940'S

Social Change

The major social change of the forties was the advent of the war, bringing with it military and civilian mobilization and the resulting state of pressure, haste, urgency, and action. This resulted in an accelerated growth of factory systems, apartments and day nurseries. Industry, with large-scale production, became less concerned with the individual needs of the worker.

The Family

The family was left mainly with two functions, love and procreation. The family seemed to be torn asunder, as fathers were absent from home, mothers were working outside the home, and children were being placed in day nurseries. Problems of young girls and young men were apparent. Attitudes toward sex changed, resulting in more frankness in regard to sex problems. This was an era of smaller families and divorce was now more acceptable as a solution to marital problems.

The family moved from traditional familism to individualism and from control by one toward an equalitarianism. As more recognition was given to tensions and hostility among family members, the family was now looked upon as a place to work out these crippling symptoms.

The Caseworker

The caseworker's skills were quickened and sharpened as, due to the times, she needed to work with more rapidity and accuracy. The emphasis of caseworkers swung to individual treatment resulting in almost exclusive emphasis on the client's *psychic problems*. The result was a tendency to neglect the family and to overlook the social situation.

Casework

Two schools of thought, the functional and diagnostic, developed and strongly influenced this era. Continued efforts to relate clients' psychic and social problems resulted in the development of psycho-social diagnosis. The interview was considered the chief tool in casework. Such principles as the relationship, the non-judgmental attitude of the caseworker, client participation, and self-determination of the client continued to crystalize.

Casework goals were directed to more selective understanding of the kernel of the problem. Three specific casework objectives were spelled out: helping clients with their environmental problems; supportive therapy; and insight therapy; or a combination of these.

Speaking of this period, Annette Garrett stated: "During the war casework probably made the most rapid advances of any period in its history, as it brought personal adjustment problems to the fore."[1]

REFERENCES

Articles

Aptekar, Herbert H.: Principles of relief giving in a family agency, *The Family, XXI:* 6:194-201, October 1940.

Arndt, Hilda C. M.: A staff evaluation of relief giving in a family agency, *The Family, XXI:* 2:54-55, April 1940.

Baer, Amelia, and East, Jane: Some problems of working mothers, *The Family, XXIII:* 10:386-391, February 1943.

Baker, Inez M.: Foster home finding, *The Family, XXVI:* 3:83-90, May 1945.

Black, Dorothy E.: Long-time or recurrent cases, *The Family, XXIV:* 8:299-306, December 1943.

---

[1] Garrett: *op. cit.,* p. 169.

————————: Long-time or recurrent cases, *The Family, XXIV:* 9:341-347, January 1944.

Bruno, Frank J.: Guide, philosopher and friend, *Journal of Social Casework, XXVII:* 1:11-13, March 1946.

Clark, Elizabeth Woodruff: A challenge to case work, *The Family, XXII:* 9:291-295, January 1942.

Cockerill, Eleanor: New emphasis on an old concept in medicine, *Journal of Social Casework, XXX:* 1:10-15, January 1949.

Day, Florence R.: Sharpening methods to meet present needs, *The Family, XXIV:* 10:363-369, February 1944.

Deutsch, Felix, M.D.: Job phobia, *Journal of Social Casework, XXVIII:* 4:131-137, April 1947.

Garrett, Annette: Historical survey of the evolution of casework, *Journal of Social Casework, XXX:* 6:218-229, June 1949.

————————: The professional base of social case work, *Journal of Social Casework, XXVII:* 5:167-174, July 1946.

————————: Transference in case work, *The Family, XXII:* 2:42-46, April 1941.

Gomberg, M. Robert: Function as a psychological concept in case work theory, *The Family, XXIV:* 2:58-64, April 1943.

Hamilton, Gordon: The underlying philosophy of social case work, *The Family, XXII:* 5:139-147, July 1941.

Hertel, Frank J.: Case work services offered by family agencies, *The Family, XXIII:* 4:129-134, June 1942.

Hollis, Florence: The techniques of casework, *Journal of Social Casework, XXX:* 6:235-244, June 1949.

Jeter, Helen R.: Wartime problems of family security, *The Family, XXIII:* 3:83-91, May 1942.

Johnson, Charles S.: New forces in family living: social reorientation, *Journal of Social Casework, XXX:* 2:47-50, February 1949.

Levey, Beatrice: The intake interview from the standpoint of supervision, *The Family, XX:* 9:289-292, January 1940.

Little, Ruby: Diagnostic recording, *Journal of Social Casework, XXX:* 1:15-19, January 1949.

Maeder, LeRoy M. A., M.D.: Diagnostic criteria—the concept of normal and abnormal, *The Family, XXII:* 6:171-179, October 1941.

————————: Generic aspects of the intake interview, *The Family, XXIII:* 1:14-23, March 1942.

Marcus, Grace F.: Family casework, in 1948, *Journal of Social Casework, XXIX:* 7:261-270, July 1948.

Martens, Elsie: Case work treatment of emotional maladjustment in marriage, *The Family, XXV:* 8:297-304, December, 1944.

Mead, Margaret: What is happening to the American family? *Journal of Social Casework, XXVIII:* 5:323-330, November 1947.

Moore, Madeline U.: Symposium on social breakdown: a plan for measurement and control, *The Family, XXI:* 9:283-288, January 1941.

Pray, Kenneth L. M.: A restatement of the generic principles of social casework practices, *Journal of Social Casework, XXVIII:* 8:283-290, October 1947.

Preston, Frances: Practical family budget counseling in private agencies, *The Family, XXIII:* 2:57-63, April 1942.

Rabinowitz, Clara: When is relief giving the role of the private agency? *The Family, XXII:* 10:348-355, February 1942.

Rasey, Mabel: Marriage counseling in a family agency, *The Family, XXIV:* 2:65-71, April 1943.

Regenburg, Jeanette: Classroom instruction in social case work, *The Family, XXI:* 4:114-119, June 1940.

Rich, Margaret E.: A modern spirit in case work, *Journal of Social Casework, XXVII:* 1:18-23, March 1946.

————————: The effects of joint administration on casework practice as seen by the private agency, *The Family, XXI:* 5:135-141, July 1940.

Ross, Helen: New forces in family living: emotional values, *Journal of Social Casework, XXX:* 2:55-58, February 1949.

Sacks, Patricia: Establishing the diagnosis in marital problems, *Journal of Social Casework, XXX:* 5:181-187, May 1949.

Scherz, Frances, and Davis, Betty Ingles: Two cases of marital difficulty handled by a family agency, *The Family, XXI:* 4:103-111, June 1940.

Schmalz, Robert M., and Freeman, Henry: Case work skills in a worker's service bureau, *The Family, XXV:* 1:19-26, March 1944.

Siebold, Janet: Helping new Americans, *Journal of Social Casework, XXX:* 2:71-77, February 1949.

Silbert, Louise: How the clients' current adjustment affects treatment possibilities, *The Family, XX:* 10:331-340, February 1940.

Sytz, Florence. The development of method in social casework, *Journal of Social Casework, XXXIX:* 3:83-88, March 1948.

————————: The unit of attention in the case work process, *Journal of Social Casework, XXVII:* 4:135-139, June 1946.

Thomas, Dorothy V.: Criteria for the giving of financial assistance in a private family agency, *Journal of Social Casework, XXVIII:* 5: 183-190, May 1947.

Waelder, Elsie M.: Casework with marital problems, *Journal of Social Casework, XXVIII:* 5:168-174, May 1947.

Waite, Florence T.: Case work—today and fifty years ago, *The Family, XXI:* 10:315-322, February 1941.

Ware, Anna Budd: Family counseling through family case work, *The Family, XXI:* 7:231-234, November 1940.

Younker, Ira M.: Family counseling in action today, *Journal of Social Casework, XXIX:* 3:106-111, March 1948.

Zurfluh, Ruth: The case work process in treatment, *The Family, XXI:* 10:329-333, February 1941.

Chapter V

AGE OF AUTOMATION, DECADE 1950-1959

*Machines which need very little help from humanity are
well past the point of mere "automation," . . . The great un-
answerable question is: What will happen to the Souls of
People?*

KEITH WHEELER

SOCIAL CHANGE

Automation and the Family

DURING the fifties, an all-out defense effort directed against the
possibility of war was in progress. This included the construction
of large scale defense plants, rearmament, and "nuclear preparedness." Many of the frustrations and deprivations of families were
associated directly with the economic steps associated with this
defense build-up. There was a nation-wide shift in the labor
market. Technological changes and automation were making formerly useful skills obsolete. *With the increased trend to specialization in industry, there tended to be less opportunity for creativity and less personal satisfaction on the job.* Family heads and
wage earners found adjustments to these changes difficult. As
a result, there was an increase in labor turnover with individuals
voluntarily leaving their jobs in an effort to obtain better positions. This was an age of insecurity and family mobility affecting
all levels of society.

As automation progressed it was believed social change would
become even more pronounced. It was as if people were being
developed to adjust to an "other-directed" world, ready to take
their places as "organization men," skilled in the soft sell.[1] Large

---

[1] J. Milton Yinger: The changing family in a changing society. *Social Casework*, XL,
October, 1959, p. 423.

cities created indoor living, factory work and sedentary occupations.

The population of some of the larger cities was expanding at approximately 400,000 per year. Each year new housing units were being built which would accommodate approximately 250,000. The equivalent number of 250,000 older units were being torn down to make way for new offices, highways, and factories. This still left the 400,000 expanded population to be absorbed "somehow." The problem was partially resolved through increased construction of apartments and one-room units.[1] Secondly, families were moving away from the large, over-crowded, rapidly changing city areas to the less anonymous suburbs. A move to the suburbs meant that the father of the family was spending less time in the home.

The expanding industrial economy brought about changes in family structure. Many boys were left without male figures with whom they could identify. Difficulties of boys and male adolescents were thought to be associated, in part, with this shift in the patterns of family interaction. As a consequence of the father's absence from the home, these boys were not learning what it was to be a man. Many new suburbs had not had time to establish social groups or lines of communication. This resulted in a form of "normlessness" and lack of values for the youth living in these suburbs. Thus these young people who were beset by confusion and a sense of being powerless attempted to create a set of values that would give them status. They improvised a "sub-culture" or "gang culture" of their own. The gang, sought initially as a refuge, in many instances became the locus of the "lonely crowd."

The urban industrial revolution seemed to be slowly undermining and disintegrating the established social structures. The speed of the industrial change was far exceeded by the rate of society's social adaptation. Ewan Clague believed that the brain that could conceive and create the atomic bomb and penicillin should also be able to envisage adaptation of social and economic living to these new conditions.

---

[1] *Ibid.*, p. 427.

The stresses and strains upon family living today are to some extent new and different, so the solutions of former times may not be useful. The situations we face require new adaptations; that is why we must diagnose the problem as it exists today and must discover solutions that may not have been tried before.[1]

There emerged largely during the fifties, two types of working classes. There were those individuals who earned their living in jobs that were sharply affected by the risks and fluctuations of business. The second class consisted of those who worked in big bureaucratic structures within which they had specialized tasks requiring specialized training and knowledge but not requiring that major risk-taking decisions be made. This was an age of mushrooming enormous bureaucracies where workers were required to feel at home with strangers, be capable of working as a team, and be able to sell themselves. The need on the job was more often for boldness than togetherness. As workers became a part of this large bureaucratic system, there was sanction of the expedient, with emphasis on a conscience that was easily bribed in order to obtain the greatest advantage for the least possible effort. Thus workers from the unskilled to the professional became a part of large organizations over which they had no control. *A new "middle working class" emerged.*

The mobile population who moved from towns or cities to the new defense plants were often disturbed by the lack of such facilities as comfortable or adequate housing, recreation, special social opportunities and personal associations, proper schooling for their children and medical care. Often moving to these areas resulted in a split of the extended families. Children were being torn away from their friends and enrolled in different schools. This migration of people from one part of the country to another also caused many families to have only tenuous ties with their relatives. As a consequence, these relatives could no longer be called upon to help with crises or to share in the responsibility of day-to-day living.

---

[1] Ewan Clague: Economic factors affecting family living, *Social Casework*, XXXIII, October, 1952, p. 324.

It seemed as if due to the increased anxiety caused by moral and ideological codes of the society and an increase in danger of accidental death through nuclear war, mechanized machinery, automobiles and airplanes, *individuals tended to seek immediate satisfactions and obtain certain experiences "prematurely" in fear they might be missed.* There was an increased emphasis on happiness as a goal in life.

THE FAMILY

Social Change and the Family

Industrial change was breaking up old culturally established structures including attitudes toward relatives, the proper roles of men and women and the training of children. As customs, beliefs, thoughts and knowledge changed, caseworkers gave more consideration to the cultural influences that had helped mold the client's life. The changing social structure fragmented family life. There was an increase in the number of diversions for adults outside the home. The pressures for conformity emphasized by movies, radio, television and advertising tended to make everyone feel that he must have what others had acquired. The expanding use of television in the homes tended to lessen verbal communication between family members. The result of rapid social change, for many, was a generalized feeling of frustration creating many tensions between family members. In fact, it appeared that society was changing so rapidly that almost every aspect of family life was being subjected to severe disturbances.

A religious resurgence was noted and continued to gain momentum into the mid and late fifties. This resurgence was characterized by an increase in church membership and physical structures rather than what some theologians referred to as "the search for spiritual verities." As a part of this movement the "Christian Family Life Education Department" of many of the major denominations experienced an expansion in activity.

The problem of finding adequate ways to blend the old and new roles of each family member into a unified single role was only partially solved. The husband's expectations of his wife were many. He expected her to play the role of sweetheart, comrade, housewife, mother, manager of the income, supplementor of the income and a representative of the family in the community. In turn, the wife expected her husband to be a sweetheart and a comrade, the breadwinner, the father, and the caretaker of the home, that he be both serious and carefree, and a good provider as well as an amorous lover.

The contemporary family patterns that were evolving had only partially filled the increasing need for husband and wife to have mutual interests and the same schedules by day and to have mutual mobility, to be together, through the years. With the acceptance of widespread divorce and the loss of the old assurance that the marriage must continue "for better or for worse" stability of family life seemed still more threatened. Divorce courts were increasingly used as a solution to marital problems.

The classifications of marital discord ranged from "deep-rooted incompatibility" to "transient and superficial conflict." There were fatherless families in which the mother sought help with employment and child care services for the children. The increase in the number of broken homes caused a general uneasiness regarding the exact nature of the role the family should play in the children's development. There were disturbed parent-child relationships ranging from severe reactions in both parent and child to the less complicated problems. *In this period of rapid social change, family problems seemed to outnumber solutions.*

There is a lack of material in available literature concerning social change as it affected the family. J. Milton Yinger stated that only in the past several years have supplementary studies been available which attempt to relate family patterns to the social structure. Prior to this time the approach to studies of the family had been primarily descriptive and practical.[1]

Economic Parents

During the fifties, money increasingly became the symbol of success and this symbol was also being used more and more as a

---

[1] Yinger: *op. cit.*, p. 419.

means of gaining status and recognition. Parents were becoming "economic" parents. They were teaching their children the paramount importance of money, buying power, and self-indulgence as consumers, and there was less emphasis on human relations and the maturing pleasures of parental responsibility. There appeared to be a shift from the importance of the production of goods to an accent on the consumption of goods. Many families were aspiring to attain higher social status. Many workers at the lower end of the income scale were conscious of their existing status in relation to the raised American standard of living and were taking steps to improve their position. The objective of the family was to develop individual personalities for in this era, it was the person with the pleasing personality, rather than the hard worker, who was receiving rewards. The major solution to the problem of how to acquire more material goods was for the mother or the wife in the family to work outside the home. In 1952, there were nine million married women in the labor force of which four million were mothers of children under the age of eighteen.[1]

Changing Family Roles

The development of new methods of disciplining children was viewed by the older generation with bewilderment. The teachings of a lifetime or of several generations were being challenged by experts and professionals whose findings were increasingly supported by scientific proof. There was a shift in the thinking of the past decades from emphasis on "major or single causation" toward the recognition of the multiple causation of behavior. There was acknowledgement of the fact that severe punishment might actually increase rather than decrease the children's desire to revolt against the mores of their parents or of society. As parents saw their children gaining more education and improved skills, parents were exposed to an impairment of their self-esteem.

At the same time, fathers and mothers were becoming more permissive parents. Signs that their children did not fit into the *group* created greater parental unhappiness than signs of a lack of indi-

---

[1] Clague: *op. cit.*, p. 326.

vidual accomplishment or creativity. Yet, at the same time, parents were setting high standards for their children and were expecting much from them.

There was a noticeable change in the father-child relationship. In the past the father was seen as being kind, but reserved and stern. The contemporary father was expected to assume many roles in his relationship with his child. He needed to awaken the emotional potential of his child, to be a teacher, an "ego ideal of masculine love," an ideal for morality, a model for social and vocational behavior, and "a stabilizing influence for solution of the oedipal conflict." He was expected to be protector, counselor and hero to the grade school child and a friend during the adolescent stage.

The adolescents in the family were under strain caused by the rapidly mounting national defense activities and the drafting of young men into the armed services. Other problems of youth involved decisions about military service, marriage, and selection of occupations. A basic uncertainty pervaded the lives of young people as they adapted to the stresses of unsettled national and international situations. Adolescents, both at home and separated from their families, were having difficulties in their work and social adjustments and were presenting anti-social behavior. There was growing concern about the increasing number of juveniles involved in acts of destruction of life and property.

Modern families seemed to be living in a greater state of tension than in the past. They had become the major "burden carrier" of a social order undergoing many rapid social changes. Through its capacity for sympathy, understanding and unlimited support, the family was expected to rehabilitate personalities that were bruised in the course of the competitive daily-work-life. The family ideal seemed to be that members of the family should have emotional stability, education, vocational skill, good health and economic security. Those families and members who did not meet this ideal were subjected to a multiplicity of pressures due to their apparent social maladjustment. Characteristics of this "companionship family" included the giving and receiving of affection; the assumption of equality of husband and wife, and the democracy of family decisions with a voice and a vote by the children. Thus, the emerging family in modern society was referred to as the "companionship family" as a result of its emphasis on *intimate interpersonal relationships as a primary function.*[1]

THE CASEWORKER

Casework Services

Caseworkers believed one of the problems involved in giving effective casework services was caused by the difficulty some clients experienced in entering into meaningful communication. In the past, if the client had not kept appointments as arranged, the caseworker had resolved the frustration by noting on the client's record the cliche, "He cannot use help." Actually, most of these clients were those most desperately in need of the help they refused. It was now believed that the client's inability to communicate was also related to the difficulty he was experiencing in better ordering his behavior and his relationships. More attention was directed to overcoming the barrier created by lack of communication between the caseworker and the client. The term, "aggressive," was used to convey the meaning of a more concerted effort, a greater "going-out," more "reaching out" to clients in an effort to help clients overcome the strong resistances they felt toward accepting casework services.

Clients were seeking help for problems of money management or housing, unemployment and their work adjustment difficulties. Adults, who were separated from their families, were having difficulties with their social relationships. Individuals with a physical disability were feeling the strain in carrying their normal responsibilities. Aging persons were encountering more problems in their employment settings and in their social adjustments. The role of the aged person in the family was changing especially in regard to living arrangements, even though there may not have been any financial problems present. Apartments left no place for members of the extended family. Increased mobility of the pres-

---

[1] Kimball Young: What strong family life means to our society, *Social Casework,* XXXIV, October, 1953, p. 327.

ent generation left older members behind. The public still appeared willing to spend more to keep a child in an institution or foster home than in his own home. Residency requirements were maintained for certain welfare services, whereas the uprooted American had no established residency.

Caseworkers discovered that clients were fearful of an agency setting and what they would "let themselves in for" by accepting casework services. It was felt that there was a need for greater understanding of "the positives and the negatives" in the clients' feelings, especially in regard to the use they would make of the assistance the caseworker had to offer. It was now believed that the client's resistance to seeking help could be broken down only through a demonstration of kindness, honesty and understanding. Thus, the client would be free to receive the benefits of the knowledge and skills the caseworker had acquired through special training. Caseworkers noted that frequently there was a testing out process in which clients tried in many ways to provoke hostility and arouse anxiety in the caseworker. It was thought that the clients did this in order to see whether their fear of a breakdown in the casework relationship would be realized. *Caseworkers developed a clearer perception of their role and the nature of the helping process. They began to interpret, and to clarify more explicitly, to clients that they offered them a chance to use constructive help so that their unsatisfactory situation might be changed.*

Marriage Counseling

The purpose of marriage counseling was to help partners cope with specific difficulties, develop the capacity to adapt to new situations, determine basic values, and meet stress and anxiety constructively.

Robert Gomberg was among the first to point out that casework services, whenever possible and when indicated, should be made available to both partners.[1] The methods by which this

---

[1] M. Robert Gomberg: Family-oriented treatment of marital problems, *Social Casework*, XXXVII, January, 1956, p. 10.

could be accomplished were explored. These methods included use of proper timing for involving the second partner and attempting to determine whether one or two caseworkers should carry the case.

Family Centered Casework

The fifties saw the revitalization of an old social work procedure, the home visit. The home visit was now seen as a means of "reaching out" to those clients who could not or would not come to the office. "It is quite clear that in our practice we have to begin to move out more firmly to certain clients . . . We are still often too hesitant about accepting a role that is essentially a preventive one."[1] It was thought that clients frequently were not in a position to evaluate their own problems or were overwhelmed by their closeness to them.

There was some difference of opinion regarding the home visit. Some felt the home visit constituted an infraction of privacy. Others believed that the home visit was a valuable casework technique in the initial social study phase of a family diagnosis. They felt it was necessary to visit the home as the central effort of the family diagnosis was to relate the behavior of a family member to the behavior of the family as a whole. The focus of the home visit was primarily on family interaction patterns, role behavior, and the physical environment and atmosphere of the home.[2]

Family inadequacies were related to personality disorder and to the prejudices of family members. It appeared that some of the most intense prejudices were frequently due to displaced hostility in a frustrating family situation. Caseworkers explored the emotional interactions in family relationships; that is, the way in which family interaction conditioned the development of the individual and the means by which these would affect the pat-

---

[1] Lionel C. Lane: Aggressive approach in preventive casework with children's problems, *Social Casework*, XXXIII, February, 1952, p. 66.

[2] Marjorie L. Behrens and Mason W. Ackerman: The home visit as an aid in family diagnosis and therapy. *Social Casework*, XXXVII, January, 1956, p. 11.

tern of the client's later living. *The distinctive purpose of social casework was to help the individual find himself in his social relationships.*

Robert Gomberg stated in 1959 that there was no diagnostic or conceptual system existing which described, assessed, or classified the family configuration.[1] Caseworkers felt that they lacked a plan or frame of reference for linking the individual components of behavior, i.e., psychological, interpersonal and social, with the behavior of significant family pairs and whole families. Heretofore, while the casework goal had been to treat the family as a whole, the caseworker had attempted to achieve this goal through working with only one family member. Viola Weiss specifically pointed out the need for a framework of knowledge of "family dynamics" when she referred to an outline[2] that had been developed which would facilitate the caseworker's focus on family dynamics rather than on individual dynamics. This outline aided in accumulating and organizing pertinent data about family dynamics.

Multi-problem Families

There was a renewed interest in helping the multi-problem families. Multi-problem families were described as those having more than their share of physical and emotional problems. They were often those families who gave evidence of having had a long history of financial dependency, poor housing, a frequently changing family unit, heavy incidence of mental illness and retardation and a pattern of behavior often violent and in conflict with accepted social standards. As caseworkers made increased efforts to reach out to these resistive clients and to establish a working relationship, new opportunities for casework services were developing.

Caseworkers were revising old approaches to helping these multi-problem families. With the renewed interest in "less hopeful" families, there was reaffirmation of the social agencies' "open door" policy for *all* clients seeking help. Caseworkers

---

1 Gomberg: *loc. cit.*

2 See copy of outline on pages 124-127.

learned that only when they had accepted the direct responsibility of doing things for and with these families that it was possible for the family to see that the caseworker was taking a direct
interest in them. The caseworker could then, at a later date, endeavor to establish a basis of understanding with the family. Caseworkers now felt that in the past they had expected too much,
too soon, in the way of progress. In some cases only demonstration, education and dealing first with the tangible problems
was used in beginning work with these families. *In certain cases,
reaching the children of multi-problem families seemed to be the
only hope of breaking the cycle of dependency.*

In the past, caseworkers had tended to bypass the multi-problem family or give service only at a point of crisis. It was now
thought that much of the caseworkers' lack of success with these
families had stemmed from their failure to establish a basis of
communication. Caseworkers felt their efforts required patience
to ferret out ego strengths and courage not to give up at signs
of client hostility. One dominant factor that stood out was the
pattern of dependency in these families. *It was found that only
as the casework focus shifted to a search for strengths on which
to build, however minimal, was there evidence of casework movement.*[1]

Private Agencies

Private social agencies were giving direct service both to individuals and to families through the practice of casework. Group
work services in the fifties sometimes extended to family groups
but the group process predominantly involving individuals with
similar problems, was rapidly expanding. However, the expansion
of group work services was not restricted to private agencies but
encompassed the broad spectrum of social service organizations.
Private social service agencies were also offering additional services by extending leadership and participating in community-
wide planning and social action to meet human needs.

[1] Kenneth Dick and Lydia J. Stand: The multi-problem family and problems of
service, *Social Casework*, XXXIX, June, 1958, p. 351.

Caseworkers were making a searching examination of social agency function and authority. The thinking was that power over community resources had been delegated to social agencies to be used for persons in need of such services. The authority of the agency was assumed by caseworkers who, by use of this formal and legitimate power, effectively participated in the casework method of helping clients with their decisions. Agency authority was seen as giving the caseworker temporary leadership responsibilities in the casework process.[1]

Many changes within private agencies were occurring. In the past, the major budget item had been the giving of economic relief. In this decade, the major budget item was staff salaries. Agency income had been derived principally from endowments and community chests, but now a third source of financial income emerged—the clients themselves. Many agencies established a fee schedule for certain services or a "sliding fee scale," based on income. However, even though clients were charged for services, many felt there was still something to "forgive" in those receiving casework services. Social agencies were still associated with the "charity" of the past, and social agencies were still raising money by appealing to pity or social fear.

Overlapping of services by different community agencies was increasing. For instance, marriage counseling services were offered by private agencies, mental health agencies, marriage counselors, psychologists, sociologists, ministers, doctors, lawyers and public welfare. There were also limited overlapping areas in the services given by family agencies and child placement agencies. The need for increased cooperation between these agencies was apparent if this duplication of services was to be eliminated. The eventual result was merging of some of these two services.

Private Practice

Agencies during the fifties questioned the "dependence" of social casework on its organized setting. They feared that the

---

[1] Elliott Studt: An outline for study of social authority factors in casework, *Social Casework*, XXXV, June, 1954, p. 321.

agency was a stumbling block to the achievement of professional dignity. However, it was felt that the organized agency offered resources and facilities beyond the command of the individual private practitioner. The agency structure made possible a united effort, a pooling of understanding and experience. In addition, through use of supervisory personnel, a concerted testing and use of accumulated knowledge and skill could be utilized. But, at the same time, the conditions of private practice were being viewed with uncritical envy and caseworkers began to enter this fertile field. This was seen by many as a major step toward professional identity.

Research

Research in family centered casework appeared to be seriously lagging behind research in psychiatry, psychology and family sociology. *In order to strengthen casework with families, additional scientific knowledge was needed to elucidate how the functioning of a family system was affected by surrounding social forces. It was believed that specific key sociological concepts needed to be added to psychodynamic concepts as these concepts had been too predominant in their influence on family casework.*

During the fifties, the focus of study was on the family constellation and the processes within the family. It was hoped that specialists in the fields of sociology, psychiatry, and anthropology would contribute to casework, and that eventually these contributions would all be integrated conceptually. It was expected that new factual material and new understanding of old ideas would shed important light on family dynamics.

Looking to the future it was hoped that scientific associates utilizing an interdisciplinary approach would develop a "human science" and raise to a higher order of abstraction data from all the behavioral sciences.

The two schools of thought in social casework, the diagnostic and the functional groups, were both being widely used in casework with less emphasis being placed on the differences of the two schools.

CASEWORK

General Methods

INTERNAL AND EXTERNAL PROBLEMS: Caseworkers attempted to offer casework services in such a manner as to provide growth-producing situations for those individuals who had not been sufficiently freed in the natural course of events to function effectively or to their own satisfaction.

> Only when the essential social medium can be weighed in his favor by the professional controls of social work or therapy is the individual freed to discover and take over his own projections as well as to feel his own spontaneous movement toward self-development.[1]

Social casework more and more turned to the core problem of the interaction between the human being and a dynamic industrial society.

Procedure and Techniques

INTAKE PROCESS: The immediate purpose of the intake process was to give the caseworker a broad picture of the person, family, and situation. No immediate attempt was made to gain knowledge of the deeper aspects required for further psycho-social diagnosis. Often the questions and comments elicited from clients in order to obtain needed facts did carry emotional implications and undertones, but no direct effort was made to reach the client's feelings in the initial phase of the contact. Limiting the use of the relationship in the initial interview made transfer to another caseworker easier if transfer was indicated.

During the intake process, it was often found that other members of the family needed to be drawn into exploration of the problem, or that more than one person needed to be included in casework services. At times, the person making the original contact was not the individual who became the client. In the interviewing situation, the caseworker's control was not a control over

---

1 Jessie Taft: A conception of the growth process underlying social casework practice, *Social Casework*, XXI, October, 1950, p. 315.

the client but rather over the interaction between caseworker and client. It was believed that this controlled interaction enabled the client to identify and use whatever motivating power he had to solve his problem.

Resistance of the client to the giving of information was still encountered in the intake interview. Because in the initial contact the primary use of the casework relationship was for exploration, caseworkers felt they needed to understand better the source of the client's resistance. It was also believed the initial interview, shaped by the worker's skill, should be directed toward channeling the client's expression of his needs in such a manner that the client became aware of some emerging order. This was to be differentiated from the various uses of the relationship in continued casework and planned treatment.

SOCIAL FUNCTIONING: Basic to the diagnostic study was the caseworker's knowledge of the individual client as well as a background of knowledge about patterns of human behavior. A diagnostic formulation entailed a careful appraisal of the client's ego functioning. The basic integrative capacity of the client's ego had to be evaluated in terms of its strength and flexibility, the effectiveness of its defenses against anxiety, and the efficiency of the ego's mechanisms in expressing realistic instinctual drives. The client's ego functioning was weighed against both the nature and strength of the client's internal drives and against the actual environmental challenge. Diagnosis was seen to be an attempt on the part of the caseworker to understand the nature of the client's difficulty in order to offer him the kind of assistance most likely to enable him to improve his *social functioning*. In addition, the caseworker needed to work with the defenses within the casework-client relationship.

The focus in diagnostic thinking was on the conscious attitudes of the client and on the reality situation. The caseworker had to accept warmly the deepest layers of the client's personality, i.e., the basic personality beneath the inappropriate surface manifestations of anxiety, otherwise the prognosis for casework treatment was considered poor. It was now widely accepted that caseworkers had to believe in the value and "basic soundness" of the client's inherent energies and drives toward maturity. *Similarly, it was recognized that the positive aspects of the defenses, as well as the individual's basic abilities and strengths were to be supported and encouraged at all times.*

THE RELATIONSHIP: Felix Biestek stated that the basic feelings and attitudes of people with psycho-social problems springs from seven fundamental needs. These basic needs, he said, elicit a definite response of feelings and attitudes in caseworkers. The seven basic human needs are: (1) The need to express feelings, both negative and positive; (2) the need for a sympathetic understanding and response to the feelings expressed; (3) the need to be recognized as a person of worth; (4) the need to be dealt with as an individual; (5) the need not to be judged a failure, a weakling, or the responsible cause of the difficulty for which the client is seeking help; (6) the need to make one's own choices and decisions concerning one's own life, and (7) the need to keep confidential information about oneself as secret as possible.[1] *The casework relationship was seen as the dynamic interaction of feelings and attitudes between the caseworker and the client which is directed toward helping the client achieve a better adjustment between himself and his environment.* Through movement in the client-caseworker relationship, the client needed to reach his particular "self" formation and self-understanding.

> For the individual, who from birth has never known any but personal relationships as his medium of development, suddenly to find himself able to project upon a person who is there for him, not using him for counter-projection, must in itself be felt as profoundly new and different, fearful perhaps, even in its potentiality for release.[2]

Thus, the *relationship* permeated all aspects of the casework process. Acceptance, non-judgmental attitude, client self-determination, and individualization were considered major qualities

---

[1] Felix Biestek, S. J.: An analysis of the casework relationship, *Social Casework*, XXXV, February, 1954, p. 60.

[2] Jessie Taft: *op. cit.*, p. 314.

of the casework relationship, and these major qualities were distinguishable from each other because each one was based on the recognition of a separate human right.

ACCEPTANCE: The keynote of the use of the "relationship" by the caseworker was "acceptance" of the person in order to facilitate understanding.

> Sometimes the caseworker finds it difficult to bear the kind and amount of anxiety that a client may show. This is understandable since overwhelming anxiety in a client creates tension in the caseworker, as well as a wish to relieve and help the person.[1]

Acceptance was considered basic to the establishment of a channel of communication and was not to be confused with warmth, permissiveness and support. The latter were specific techniques employed by the caseworker in the relationship once the treatment goal had been defined.

NON-JUDGMENTAL ATTITUDE: In 1953, a writer stated that in reviewing thirty years of social work literature, not one single article was found devoted explicitly to a discussion of the caseworker's non-judgmental attitude in the client-caseworker relationship. He said that the following propositions were contained in a definition of the non-judgmental attitude: (1) It is based upon a fundamental human right; (2) it is necessary for effective casework; (3) it is not indifferent to social and moral values; the caseworker does evaluate objectively the attitudes, standards, or actions of the client; (4) it is based on a conviction of the importance of a non-judgmental attitude; (5) it involves both thought and feeling elements; and (6) the non-judgmental attitude is transmitted to the client.[2]

SELF-DETERMINATION: Implicit in the self-determination of the client was the client's right and need to be free to make his own decisions and his own choices. Therefore, the caseworker had the duty to respect the client's right of self-determination; to refrain

---

[1] Frances Scherz: Intake: concept and process, *Social Casework*, XXXIII, June, 1952, p. 233.

[2] Biestek: *loc. cit.*

from any direct or indirect interference with this right; and to help the client positively to exercise his right. However, the caseworker must temper this with consideration of the limitations: the client's capacity for positive and constructive self-determination; the framework of social and moral good; standards of the community; law and authority; as well as the limitations of the function of the social agency.

Caseworkers recognized that within human nature there was an irrepressible need to resist outside domination at whatever ultimate cost. They also recognized that the client had a largely unused capacity to change and strengthen his control over his own destiny. This capacity to change was more apt to occur when a situation was encountered which disrupted the habitual patterns of behavior. The disruption of these patterns released the underlying growth tendencies allowing the formation of a newly integrated self. It was during periods of crisis that the individual was brought to the necessity of enlarging his integrative processes. That is, clients tended to change more at points of crises or stress when the pressure for further development became strong enough to overcome the fear of change and of disruption of old ways.

Jessie Taft, remarking on the reorganization of self, stated that in order to believe in the possibility of giving help or receiving help in any fundamental way, it was necessary to believe that there existed a natural inherent impulse in individuals which directed them toward better organization of self—regardless of how blocked or confused the impulse might be.[1] It was considered a truism that the client needed to want help in better organization of self; otherwise it would not be possible for the helper to function.

CLARIFICATION AND CONFRONTATION: During the fifties, caseworkers discovered that in a high incidence of cases, clients were those with character disorder, sometimes referred to as personality pattern (or trait) disturbance, or sociopathic personality. These clients handled their anxiety (which seemed to be instinc-

---

[1] Jessie Taft: *op. cit.,* p. 311.

tual rather than arising out of inner conflict) by impulsive "acting out" behavior rather than repression and neurotic symptom formation. Their strong instincts were expressed by aggressiveness, restlessness, and hyperactivity, combined with a weak ego and very few defenses to resist the impulse of immediate gratification of their needs. *Caseworkers grew concerned over the high incidence of cases in their caseload of clients whose difficulties stemmed from character disorder, and the "acting out" that was evidenced in such disorders.*

Offering casework services to clients with character disorders required the use of specific casework techniques, such as supporting ego strengths, and giving firm direction, environmental manipulation, clarification of the current reality, and confrontation of current behavior. The client who had never identified with consistent, mature behavior characterized by a genuine concern in regard to the outcome and predictability of his acts, was given the opportunity for such an experience in the casework relationship.

Treatment Goals

PREVENTIVE APPROACH: Caseworkers felt it was essential that public recognition be given the fact that people in need required not only economic assistance but individualized attention in order to deal with their highly complicated problems. They also believed that skilled counseling, prior to a point of crisis, could help to keep many families intact.

MODIFICATION OF ADAPTIVE PATTERNS: The caseworker needed to incorporate an understanding of character structure, personality development and the dynamics of interpersonal relations, as well as the relation of these psychological factors to psycho-social diagnosis, to the casework method, and to differentiated treatment goals. Thus, during and following the diagnostic study and the formulation of an agreed upon goal, casework treatment was used as an systematic effort to influence constructively the client's attitude and behavior. The caseworker also utilized all the outer resources of the environment and the community which might be of value in the problem-solving endeavor.

Frances Scherz defined the two main treatment aims in casework as: (1) the maintenance or reinforcement of current social functioning, and (2) the modification of behavior and attitudes in relation to current social functioning.[1] However, Sidney J. Berkowitz felt it undervalued casework to refer to treatment as "maintaining adaptive patterns," when it resulted in helping people control some of their destructive impulses or to manage their environment more effectively. "The difference [of casework] from one case to another is of degree rather than of kind."[2] In other words, all casework treatment had as its goal the modification of adaptive patterns *as well as* the maintenance or reinforcement of current social functioning. Thus, the treatment process operated through the purposeful working relationship where the need and the problem were met in ways that strengthened the individual and family potentialities to facilitate increased self-direction and more satisfying living. *The emphasis in casework was on fostering every inner strength of the client toward the goal of finding his own solution of the problem.*

SUMMARY OF THE 1950'S

Social Change

The major social change of the fifties was the introduction of automation. This was an era of large bureaucracies and big business. Automation and industrial expansion required that labor have increased specialized training and scientific knowledge. The trend to conformity meant less personal creativeness and fewer personal satisfactions on the job. One of the major problems of the times was how to make the necessary social adjustments to an ever-expanding industrial urban revolution which was linked with the movement of an expanding urban society to the suburbs. This was an era of an increasingly mobile society. The threats to survival posed by possible nuclear war meant individuals were

---

[1] Frances Scherz: Criteria for defining program and emphasis in the family agency
Social Casework, XXXII, March, 1951, p. 107.

[2] Sidney J. Berkowitz: Some specific techniques of psycho-social diagnosis and treatment in family casework, *Social Casework,* XXXVI, November, 1955, p. 399.

beginning to seek immediate satisfactions. The trends to consumption meant an increased emphasis on obtaining material things.

The Family

The family was the major burden carrier of rapid social change and the expectations of the family were to rehabilitate its members from the stress and strain of daily living. Time-honored customs, beliefs, and values were changing, thus creating a change in attitudes toward family members. Roles of family members were altered and they were also expected to assume more roles. The family was becoming more fragmented, with a resulting increase of pressures on adolescents, the aging, and children. Multi-problem families were seen as having more than their share of physical and emotional problems, with resultant financial dependency, poor housing, mental illness, and increased violence. Husbands and wives were attempting to work out a pattern of mutual interests and schedules in the day and to adjust to and develop mutual patterns of mobility through the years.

The Caseworker

Caseworkers again emphasized the use of the home visit and "the family approach," with increased focus on the social situation. There was a noticeable growth in the number of men entering the field of social work. Caseworkers used more "reaching out" techniques in an effort to help families to re-establish communication. They turned again to sociology and to the social sciences and directed their efforts towards finding methods of combining psychological and sociological problems and solutions. They were dealing with the highly complicated problems which resulted from the interaction of human beings in a *dynamic industrial society*. Caseworkers moved into private practice in a continued search for professional identity.

Casework

Casework was focused on fostering strengths, with emphasis on self-direction in an attempt to help individuals live satisfying lives. Casework goals were to improve or maintain social functioning.

OUTLINE FOR FAMILY DYNAMICS

I. Family Identifying Data
   A. List of persons in household by family role, name, and age
   B. Relatives out of home (similar data to above)
   C. Significant family dates, e.g., marriages, divorces, births, deaths
   D. Social and economic facts: race, religion, occupation and income, school level of children and adults, military status, housing and neighborhood, cultural background, group affiliations, contacts with other social agencies

II. Agency Contacts
   A. Date of initial contact or contacts
   B. By whom referred, reason for referral, relationship of referring person to family
   C. Family member who initiated contact, reason for contact
   D. Length and frequency of contact of each person being seen, how many caseworkers are involved, locale of contacts (home or office)

III. Current Social and Psychological Situation
   A. Pertinent elaboration of identifying data; physical descriptions of family members, home, and neighborhood; cultural patterns
   B. Family functioning, including:
      1. Housekeeping and living arrangements
      2. Eating and food preparation
      3. Money handling
      4. Discipline
      5. Recreation
      6. Family routines and rituals, if any
      7. Family values

C. Description of each client in terms of:
1. Problem as client sees it, verbalized feelings about problems
2. Client's current life adjustment, including work, family, health, and recreation
3. Nature of important relationships in client's life, including feelings about these persons
4. Symptoms
5. Evaluation of client by other family members
6. Client-worker relationship, including worker's observations

D. If information is available and pertinent, similar descriptions of other family members

IV. Social History
A. History of each parent
B. Family history

V. Present Transactions
A. Cultural description of family from point of view of community, including an evaluation of identifying data
B. Degree and kinds of environmental stresses upon family and their effects upon family integration; the precipitating stress
C. Nature and degree of cultural and subcultural conflicts, if any, in terms of:
1. Differences of cultural values within family
2. Members acceptance of family values
D. Characteristic handling of social roles by family members:
1. Roles accepted, rejected, and so on
2. Complementarity of roles or refusal to accept complementarity, giving reasons
3. Disparity between explicit (conscious) roles and implicit (unconscious) roles
4. Evaluation of failures to accept social roles
a. Internal stress (inner conflict)
b. External stress (not permitted to play role)
5. Culturally inappropriate roles

     6. Evaluation of individual's role playing by other family members

     7. Deviations for characteristic handling of roles

     8. Attempts at re-equilibration

  E. Dominance pattern:

     1. Stability or fluctuation

     2. Rebellion against hierarchy of dominance

  F. Family goals:

     1. Common goals, if any

     2. Appropriateness of goals

     3. Success in achievement

     4. Willingness of members to sacrifice personal satisfaction to family goal

  G. Degree and kinds of satisfactions family provides to individual members

VI. Historical Perspective of Family Transactions

VII. Psychodynamics of Individual Members

  A. Characterological descriptions:

     1. Main and subsidiary traits and/or outstanding symptoms

     2. Areas of inhibition and substitutes for inhibited areas

  B. Basic conflicts

  C. Developmental dynamics

  D. Diagnosis

VIII. Family Treatment

  A. Casework goals for family as unit:

     1. What various members want agency to provide

     2. Prediction of optimal family adjustment to be expected through casework treatment:

       a. Modifications of individual behavior necessary to attain goal

       b. Effect of behavioral modifications upon family transactions

       c. Problems modifications might create in family equilibrium

B. Casework techniques needed to achieve modifications:
1. How many clients, how many workers, in what settings
2. Specific techniques to be employed and degree of their use, e.g., guidance, exploitation of defenses, insight
3. Timing of various techniques.

REFERENCES

Articles

Behrens, Marjorie L., and Ackerman, Mason W., M.D.: The home visit as an aid in family diagnosis and therapy, *Social Casework, XXXVII:* 1:11-19, January 1956.

Berkowitz, Sidney J.: Some specific techniques of psychosocial diagnosis and treatment in family casework, *Social Casework, XXXVI:* 9:399-406, November 1955.

Biestek, Felix P. S. J.: An analysis of the casework relationship, *Social Casework, XXXV:* 2:57-61, February 1954.

————: The non-judgmental attitude, *Social Casework, XXXIV:* 6:235-239, June 1953.

————: The principle of client self-determination, *Social Casework, XXXII:* 9:369-375, November 1951.

Clague, Ewan: Economic factors affecting family living, *Social Casework, XXXIII:* 8:324-329, October 1952.

Dick, Kenneth and Strand, Lydia J.: The multi-problem family and problems of service, *Social Casework, XXXIX:* 6:349-355, June 1958.

English, O. Spurgeon, M.D.: The psychological role of the father in the family, *Social Casework, XXXV:* 8:323-329, October 1954.

FSAA Committee Report: The content of family social work, *Social Casework, XXXVII:* 7:319-326, July 1956.

Gomberg, M. Robert: Family-oriented treatment of marital problems, *Social Casework, XXXVII:* 1:3-10, January 1956.

Gregory, Jean L.: The generic and specific aspects of a family casework program, *Social Casework, XXXII:* 7:284-291, July 1950.

---

[1] Viola Weiss and Russell Monroe: *A Framework for Understanding Family Dynamics:* Part 1, pp. 7-8.

Hanford, Jeanette: The place of the family agency in marital counseling, *Social Casework, XXXIV:* 6:247-253, June 1953.

Hill, Reuben: Are we expecting too much of families? *Social Casework, XXXII:* 4:153-155, April 1951.

Hoffman, Mary Ellen: An analysis of clients with character disorders, *Social Casework, XXXVII:* 3:126-132, March 1957.

Hollis, Florence: The relationship between psycho-social diagnosis and treatment, *Social Casework, XXX:* 2:67-74, February 1951.

Jay, L. Roney: Social stresses on the family, *Social Casework, XXXIX:* 2-3:150-156, February-March 1958.

Krug, Othilde, M.D.: The dynamic use of the ego functions in casework practice, *Social Casework, XXXVI:* 10:443-450, December 1955.

Lane, Lionel: 'Aggressive' approach in preventive casework with children's problems, *Social Casework, XXXIII:* 2:61-64, February 1952.

Marcus, Grace F.: The advance of social casework in its distinctive social usefulness, *Social Casework, XXXVI:* 9:391-398, November 1955.

Mitchell, Celia Brody: Family interviewing in family diagnosis, *Social Casework, XL:* 7:381-384, July 1959.

Scherz, Frances H.: Criteria for defining program and emphasis in the family agency, *Social Casework, XXXII:* 3:107-114, March 1951.

———————: Intake: concept and process, *Social Casework, XXXIII:* 6:233-240, June 1952.

Sottong, Philipp, M.D.: The dilemma of the parent as culture bearer, *Social Casework, XXXVI:* 7:302-306, July 1955.

Studt, Elliot: An outline for study of social authority factors in casework, *Social Casework, XXV:* 6:231-238, June 1954.

Taft, Jessie: Conception of the growth process underlying social casework practice, *Social Casework, XXXI:* 8:311-318, October 1950.

Warren, Effie: Treatment of marriage partners with character disorders, *Social Casework, XXXVIII:* 3:118-126, March 1957.

Weiss, Viola and Monroe: A framework for understanding family dynamics, Part 1, *Social Casework, XL:* 1:3-9, January 1959.

Yinger, J. Milton: The changing family in a changing society, *Social Casework, XL:* 8:419-428, October 1959.

Young, Kimball: What strong family life means to our society, *Social Casework, XXXIV:* 8:323-329, October 1953.

Chapter VI

THE SPACE AGE, THE EARLY SIXTIES

Sometimes I wonder what will become of me
My heart yearns for permanence which never can be
I do not know a real face any more
And my compassion is misplaced . . .

Loneliness BY CLARK E. MOUSTAKES

SOCIAL CHANGE

The Space Age and the Family

WITH THE SIXTIES came a new attitude and awareness of the time-space relationship as a result of space travel and shrinking world boundaries. Man's wits seemed to have all but outwitted him by creating a threat of total destruction. A major concern of this era was man's displacement in a world of science and technology. Neither the social nor physical scientists were able to provide an explanation of man's relation to the universe and the reasons and purposes of his existence which could be accepted as "emotionally meaningful" by a significant segment of the population. Man's feelings of mistrust directed toward his fellow human beings, and his uncertainty about "tomorrow" and "survival" created increased anxiety about the future.

Charlotte Towle, in referring to "these civilized-primitive times," spoke of the high value placed on individuality in the past which had resulted in trust and worship of leadership and how this adulation now co-existed with a high value on conformity. "This is the age of the corporate image—the age of the adaptable conscience. Loss of hope has led to defenses against anxiety which take many forms."[1]

---

[1] Charlotte Towle: Social work: Cause and function, 1961, *Social Casework*, XLII, October, 1961, p. 285.

Correlated with the scientific and technological expansion was the social evolution of man. Changes in culture were apparent and class structures became more complex. There was evidence of an imbalance between the requirements of society and the actual day to day living patterns of its members. The patterns of society were changing more rapidly than the actual life patterns and behavioral characteristics of its members. The concern of social workers was that man tended to internalize and incorporate these long periods of social disorganization. Herbert Stroup cited Erich Fromm's referral to man's spiritual displacement in a depersonalized society as an "alienation," a loneliness, a self-estrangement, anonymity, means-centeredness, indifference, isolation, powerlessness, meaninglessness, and disenchantment. Continued efforts to gain an increased understanding of the inner forces of the lives of man uncovered only incredulity, aimlessness, rootlessness, dehumanization, insecurity, irrationality, resentment and aloneness which dominated his life. Man was referred to as being alone in the universe, in society and to himself.

> Instead of heightening individuality, current society depresses it . . . this is true of economic relations—man's political, educational, recreational, familial and religious experiences. Perhaps only the family, as if in romantic revolt, has established an effective counteraction to the major trends in society.[1]

Significantly, although considerable attention was paid to the subject of "conformity," comparatively little was written about man's "loneliness" in the current space age society of the sixties.

During this period, the professions of psychoanalysis, psychiatry, psychology and sociology were contributing to the increased understanding of the importance and significance of family life. There was no question that now, more than ever before, it was necessary to work for correction of policies and practices which violated family living and which were imbedded in the larger institutions of society. *There appeared to be an increased aware-*

---

[1] Herbert Stroup: A historical explanation of alienation, *Social Casework*, XLII, March, 1961, p. 107.

*ness of the interdependence of the fate of the individual and of.
the group.*

THE FAMILY

Social Change and the Family

Cultural patterns and values were changing and evolving for
all groups in society. Communication was heightened and has-
tened by advertising and by more rapid dissemination of news.
As a result of the rising standard of living, many families were
willing to spend more time to secure material goods and less time
in pursuit of leisure and recreational activities. The "on-the-
move-American-family" had become a mobile unit in a fluid
society. There was a growing recognition that the American
society would need to work out new patterns of living if it was
to successfully cope with automation in industry and in the home.

The extension of world boundaries appeared to be associated
with increasing geographic mobility. In the United States, the
accelerated mobility of the population often resulted in the
"stranded" nuclear family. The American family was on the
move both voluntarily and involuntarily. An ever increasing
mobile population demanded the development of new theories
and practices to cope with the mobile individual's disengagement
from activity and from social relationships. By choice there was
a trend away from farms and toward industrial employment. Similarly, there was a movement from urban areas to suburban areas
to escape from unsatisfactory housing and in search of communities with better living conditions. Involuntary moves were
caused by an expanding complex industrial development, construction of freeways, public facilities, and by continued attempts
to eliminate overcrowded districts in large urban areas. In re-
locating these families away from overcrowded blight areas into
public housing, it was necessary to consider not only the economic and physical aspects of city renewal plans, but also "human
renewal" as well. When city planning did not give consideration
to the people involved, families often had to move to nearby
areas already overcrowded, thus creating more blight. It soon
became evident that more consideration also needed to be given

to providing larger family units as well as the small family units.[1] It was estimated that more than 150,000 families a year were being involuntarily displaced.[2]

Automation and industrialization shifted segments of the working class into the middle class. One aspect of this mass movement was the relative disappearance of the common laborer. Many of the wealthy no longer made a conspicuous display of their affluence thus making it increasingly difficult to differentiate between this class and the middle class.

Women constituted one-third of the labor market. This meant that approximately twenty-three million women were working in industry.[3] For numerous reasons, many women were in low paying jobs. Some were marginal workers, those women who sought employment in low paying occupations. Some of these workers entered the field of low paying employment due to lack of education or training, because they were not as mobile as men, or because they were members of certain racial and nationality groups. Women in employment represented two age groups. The younger group (those prior to or early in their marriage) were replacing older workers because industrial machines demanded the services of a younger person. The other age group representd those workers re-entering the labor market during middle age Some women sought employment both during the ups and downs of the business cycle thus taking advantage of good employment conditions when they existed, and during the periods of temporary recession they sought jobs to provide or supplement family income.

The American family is ultimately a self-liquidating one. It is expected that when children reach maturity they will leave the home of their parents and start families of their own. In this age of mobility, many of the young felt rootless. They consid-

---

[1] Dorothy S. Montgomery: Relocation and its impact on families, *Social Casework*, XLI, October, 1960, p. 402.

[2] *Ibid.*

[3] Mildred Rendl-Marcus: Women in the labor force, *Social Casework*, XLI, June, 1960, p. 298.

ered themselves alienated from their parents. Also, parents needed ties to their own past which they no longer had. The aging
were exposed to such "new ideas" as nuclear warfare, automation,
television, satellites, skin-divers and astronauts in outer space. To
face these changes alone meant loneliness and an increased fear
of growing old in many instances. A great majority of the aged
were not working, were without adequate income, social security,
good health, private pensions, medical or hospital insurance. In
this current period of abundance, it seemed easy to forget what
it meant to be hungry and in want. Plans for exploration of
potentialities of learning in later years of life were developing, for,
to be functionless, even *with* economic comfort meant to "eat
your heart out."[1] An ever increasing mobile population was focus-
ing the need for new practices and theories to cope with the
mobile individual's disengagement from activity and from social
relationships.

One of the problems related to social adjustment was in the
area of changing behavior patterns. The individual's methods of
adjusting, his behavior patterns that were causing problems were
being diagnosed as "character disorders," rather than the previously used term "neurosis." This group included people who were
having difficulty with authority, who were destructive and dis-
honest. These phenomena were believed to be due in part to
changes in the value system, a lack of direction, a feeling of
uncertainty, and a questioning—about the meaning of existence.
Some experts traced the causes of these manifestations to the
parents' insecurity in relation to child rearing, while still other
experts pointed to the methods of education that were being used
during the past decades.

THE CASEWORKER

Values

In the early sixties, more caseworkers became involved in working with groups, and the group process increasingly became one

---

[1] Esther Lazarus: The influence of the social structure on casework practice with the
aging, *Social Casework*, XLII, May-June, 1961, p. 250.

of the caseworker's basic working tools. A rapidly growing number of agencies was now doing group work with families. However, this meant that caseworkers needed to have a knowledge of the dynamics of family life, the significance of social and family role relations and skill in using interactional interviewing techniques. Social caseworkers were remembering one of the historic principles summed up in the phrase "people are fashioned by the milieu in which they live."[1] They were using their knowledge of class culture with particular emphasis on the different sub-cultures. Caseworkers recognized that clients coming from these various sub-cultures would have a background of different experiences which had been internalized and which in turn were reflected by attitudes. A viewpoint emerged in casework which saw each client as having his own conception of his relation to natural and supernatural forces.[2] A client might believe man good, bad, or some of both. He might believe that one can change, or is unchangeable, is submissive to, in harmony, or can master natural forces. It was recognized that in some sub-cultures individuals alternate between excitement and monotonous routine and that some families had strong "built-in" attitudes of distrust and resistiveness.

Caseworkers were increasingly aware that it was necessary to recognize not only the difference in cultural value orientations of clients but also to have an understanding of their own middle class values lest they unconsciously impose their own values on the client. They realized that their orientation might differ from that of their clients in relation to social behavior, patterns of family living, personal hygiene and appearance, dating, educational aspirations or job selection, personal possessions and property, aggressiveness and sexuality. As a result, caseworkers were exerting more effort to establish a better understanding between the clients and themselves in order to prevent their own attitudes from creating an impediment in the casework relationship.

---

[1] Shirley Cooper: New trends in work with parents: Progress or change? *Social Casework*, XLII, July, 1961, p. 342.

[2] Shirley C. Hellenbrand: Client value orientation: Implications for diagnosis and treatment, *Social Casework*, XLII, April 1961, p. 163.

The authority which had been delegated to caseworkers because of their technical knowledge and by community sanction was referred to as "a form of power" which they were to exercise to achieve certain ends. Casework treatment, therefore, was considered by some to be one of society's alternative ways of exercising social control over persons who manifested deviant behavior.

With the trend toward the use of the group process, new casework recording methods had to be developed in order to summarize group interaction, both verbal and non-verbal communications. The continued development of the group method was a vital factor in bringing about re-examination of the procedures of individual casework.

Family Centered Casework

The casework emphasis on intrapsychic forces that existed during the fifties now appeared to have given way to a greater interest in the impact of the environment on the individual's personality and to the connection between an individual's adaptation and his family experiences. This expanding emphasis meant working simultaneously with the troubled individual and his milieu, especially the immediate family group, the involved extended family members and "significant others." The emphasis was now on knowing the whole person, to unite or bring together the psychic threads that connect a person's inner, interpersonal self and social experiences. Family experiences involved the family system, a complicated world of inter-relationships with three sub-groups, the marital relationship, the parent-child relationship and sibling relationships.

In family centered casework, caseworkers were expected to know the range and needs of the members of the family group and to determine what the major needs were. They had to recognize the power positions of the family and to recognize that members might attempt to block the casework effort. In addition, they needed to evaluate resources and strengths of family members that could be turned into assets in the helping task. The relationships of the family to other institutions in the community also had to be determined and evaluated.[1] Transference and counter-transference reactions occurring in the group process had to be recognized. When "multi-clients" were involved, the caseworker was expected to be task oriented by keeping family goals in focus.

The focus of family centered casework was on interpersonal relationships—the links between individuals. As the caseworkers and family members worked together, the links between past and present difficulties as well as the internal conflicts and social functioning of each individual became apparent. Tensions due to individual striving and group pressures became obvious.

It was considered a truism that the most expert help for children was practically useless unless there was a concomitant change in the family as a whole and particularly in the parents. It was found that when parents were included in the casework services, they developed a sense of responsibility (as opposed to guilt) toward their children. The trend in thinking was that a child should combine, in a creative way, models of behavior from many persons in his life. It could be considered pathology if a child was merely a reflector of the behavior of his parents.

In the past decades, clients diagnosed as "character disorder" had been considered untreatable, both because they did not respond to efforts to free them from guilt and anxiety, and because they were relatively free of conscious guilt and placed the blame for their difficulties on others. It was now considered that clients with this diagnosis were treatable. To help clients with character disorder to grow, caseworkers first had to accept the client's need to be "given to" as these clients required direct guidance. This was based on the assumption that if in the beginning of treatment the client's controls were further released, the client could be driven to panic. This procedure of "giving to" was referred to as "therapeutic use of permissiveness." After giving recognition and empathy, the caseworker then had to be available for "release of the client's feelings." The final step was

---

[1] Otto Pollak and Donald Brieland: The midwest seminar on family diagnosis and treatment, *Social Casework*, XLII, July, 1961, p. 320.

directed toward clarification, confrontation, re-education and helping the client establish control for better social functioning and ego organization.

It was recognized, however, that there were clients with character disorder who needed external controls, and that this was especially true when their behavior created danger to themselves or others. In these cases, firmness was considered to provide an ego supportive experience for the client. Firmness was thought to be an aid in helping the individual toward a shift in adaptive and protective mechanisms which would result in a better mobilization of self in relation to the problem.

Marriage Counseling

Diagnosis in marriage problems focused on gaining a clear understanding of the individual diagnosis of each partner coupled with an understanding of the marital interaction between them. With this diagnostic thinking, the trend in interviewing was toward joint interviews designed to determine marital interaction, the degree of cooperation or breakdown in their relationship with its resulting conflict, resignation, or contesting the legitimacy of each other's wishes.

Chronic, Hard Core, Multi-problem Families

Caseworkers found that families with long periods of social dependency, referred to as "multi-problem" and "hard core" families, were apathetic, destructively aggressive, immature, and socially and economically maladjusted. These families were discovered to have problems of poor housekeeping, often being chronically delinquent in rent payments. Marital maladjustments frequently involved the police. Many of these families also revealed a history of chronic illness. Elderly couples, alone and ill, but not ill enough for hospitalization were among this group as well as many juveniles who manifested troublesome behavior problems.

A large percentage of "families with problems" were found to stem from the lower class sub-culture. Some of the characteristics of this sub-culture were spelled out as: (1) the nature of their work is unskilled or semi-skilled, seasonal, cyclical, monotonous, and involving long hours; (2) limited schooling; (3) poor housing; (4) families of the three or four stem type, the result of frequent separation, desertion or divorce; (5) a female based household, and frequent serial mating; (6) the peer group's superceding the family as the primary reference group; (7) a carpe diem philosophy,* (8) deep seated mistrust of authority figures transmitted by attitudes, deeds and words from adults to their children, and (9) a tendency toward self-centeredness, suspicion of and hostility toward institutional controls and suspicion among members of the group brought about by divorces, frequent separations and desertions.[1]

Interest in use of the home visit continued. During the past decades, particularly the forties when the emphasis was on the client's internal stresses, the home visit had fallen into disfavor. With the renewed interest in social phenomena, the home visit added new dimension to the caseworker's understanding of the family interaction. This added understanding increased the possibility of the caseworker and family developing a greater feeling of friendliness and trust. Permanent "cures" in casework were not expected. This meant the caseworker was considered a resource and that the return of the client for casework services was not an indication of a casework failure. When clients returned for further services, it was now felt that the client had been served well. However, caseworkers were still concerned over "drop outs" from their caseloads.

Social Science

In an attempt to describe the social world accurately and in order to foster theory development, the social scientist was raising many hypothetical questions. In contrast to social casework, social science is more concerned with theory and research and consequently is more centered in areas of abstraction. The social

---

* A philosophy of "live today, let tomorrow take care of itself."

[1] Hellenbrand: *loc. cit.*

sciences, particularly sociology, were growing closer to social work as evidenced by jointly sponsored professional meetings.

Some caseworkers felt that they had little in common with the findings of social science. They thought that theory and research were out of touch with reality, and that the vocabulary seemed "strange and unintelligible."[1] One writer warned lest the flirtation with social sciences become a "historical romance" and that "we may have committed ourselves too deeply to the pursuit of knowledge for us to pause to seek wisdom," and "our current concern with conceptualization is part of an insistent and tenacious drive for respectability which seems to characterize the culture of contemporary social work."[2]

There was general agreement that the solution to the problem of assimilating knowledge from social science was to be found in incorporating the new socio-cultural insights with the present psychological base of casework. The apparent need was for the field of casework to develop a framework that would include social science theory as well as behavioral theory.

Definition of Casework

The following definition integrates psychodynamics and sociodynamics into a workable definition of casework, but the length and wordiness of the definition emphasizes the need for more unifying concepts.

> Social casework is a method of social work which intervenes in the psycho-social aspects of a person's life to improve, restore, maintain or enhance his social functioning by improving his role performance. Intervention occurs when the person, or members of his group or his community, realize that his role performance is hampered or threatened. The intervention takes place through a professional relationship between the worker and the person, and also between the worker and other individuals whose interaction with the person affects his role

---

[1] Mary J. McCormick: The role of values in social functioning, *Social Casework*, XLII, February, 1961, p. 74.

[2] Morton I. Teicher: The culture of concepts, *Social Casework*, XLII, December, 1961, p. 491.

performance. Since social functioning is the product of inter-action among intra-psychic, somatic, and social forces, social casework involves assessing the internal and social factors which impair or threaten the person's role performance and helping him to find and use the somatic, psychic and social resources at his disposal, to eliminate or reduce malfunction and to enhance functioning in social roles.[1]

Changing Terminology

Some disagreement over the nature, the dimensions, and even the terminology of family centered casework began to arise among caseworkers. This disagreement involved both the concept of family diagnosis and family treatment. *Caseworkers were being encouraged to explore new approaches to diagnosis and to develop new techniques of helping.*

During the past decades, Mary Richmond and Gordon Hamilton made efforts to formulate a social casework terminology. The problem at hand, during the early sixties, was how to integrate psychiatric and sociological terminology. It was recognized that the psychiatric nomenclature had only limited use in developing casework classifications. It was not oriented toward the individual and his psycho-physical processes, the person-in-his-situation, nor the person's problems in social functioning. The beginning of planning to develop a "new" professional vocabulary appeared to be under way.

During the early sixties, with casework aimed at enhancing an individual's social functioning, caseworkers had to take into consideration the relationship between the client and his social system. The following terms represent the means by which multi-dimensional factors were combined into a constellation of related concepts: *A social system* was considered an assemblage of related parts, each affecting the other through interaction. The parts were termed roles, personality, or a family member. *Social functioning* was the sum of the individual's activities in inter-action. Social functioning, social role, role performance meant

---

[1] Jeanette Regensburg: Implications for the practice of social casework, *Social Case-work*, XLI, January, 1960, p. 14.

not only surface manifestations of behavior, but also determinants of behavior, such as physical endowments and ego functioning, which included both intellectual and emotional and social factors.

SOCIAL ROLE, the unit in social functioning, was considered to be a set of activities or behavior patterns belonging together. That is, social role is a person's organized pattern or mode of behavior, fashioned by the status or functions he carried in relation to one or more persons. Social types were considered one aspect of social role such as the "different one." Social type was an old concept now changed, in order to be both more specific and more dynamic and including social as well as psychological dimensions. "Social types are descriptions of personality in terms of both situation and organism and their interaction."[1] The growing emphasis in the profession on social functioning suggested the need for a classification of personality that would include social roles and types. *Value* was the abstract ideal of what was expected of the individual. *Stress* was the situation that threatens performance in social roles. The *problem* was the impairment in the role performance due to the individual's response to stress. *Balance* was a key element in man's relations with other men, his adaptability to fit behavior to new uses, the striving to function satisfactorily in a complex society.[2] *Control* was a social or psychological process by which the ideal was achieved and enforced.

Another current problem was that of finding a system for classifying various kinds of problem entities in the person-in-the-situation configuration. The caseworker was seen as acquiring three types of data—(1) in regard to the individual person, (2) his cultural and value orientation, and (3) environmental data. Diagnostic and treatment classification systems were needed. It was evident that there was a lack of typologies of problems and personalities as linked to situations.

The efforts to apply role theory to casework and to integrate it with ego theory presented problems. In developing new ter-

---

[1] Max Siporin: The concept of social types in casework and theory, *Social Casework*, XLI, May, 1960, p. 235.

[2] McCormick: *op. cit.*, p. 71.

minology, an analogy was made to redecorating. It was cautioned that in redecorating, care needed to be taken not to throw out all the old furniture, there being a need for integration of the old and the new. It was felt that many concepts could be properly related to each other if a higher order of concept could be devised to include them.

CASEWORK

General Methods

THE GROUP: The trend in casework during this part of the sixties was directed toward group work with the whole family in family centered sessions. Group work with the family was based on generalized assumptions about the interpersonal links between the individual and recognized family processes, the dynamics of family life.

"When the focus is on interaction, neither the individual nor the group is submerged, but the group medium is utilized in the interests of the particular individual."[1]

NEW DIMENSIONS: Although there was a recognition that the client or group was the product of interacting psychological, somatic, social and cultural factors, the development of an integrated theoretical framework had not as yet been attained. There was a need for further development of the *inter-relationship* of the psychological, somatic, social and cultural factors. It was hoped that clarification of the complexities of this *inter-relationship* would lead to a resolution of the many problems attendant to the integration of individual casework efforts with the use of the group method.

Procedure and Techniques

INTAKE INTERVIEW: The initial interview was regarded and treated as a potential for doing preventive casework. The purpose of the interview was to gain a clearer understanding between the applicant and the caseworker as they explored together what

---

[1] Celia Brody Mitchell: The use of family sessions in the diagnosis and treatment of disturbances in children, *Social Casework*, XLI, June, 1960, p. 284.

the client wanted, what he actually expected, and what was realizable.

Further, with the caseworker bearing in mind that the applicant does not chose a particular helper relationship with a particular caseworker, reciprocal role expectations were clarified. There had been some misconceptions in regard to the reciprocal roles of the client and the caseworker in past decades. Now the caseworker was more involved in engaging the applicant in wanting to use casework help and exploring the client's understanding and willingness to try the "suggested ways of getting at his problem." The emphasis was on the caseworker and the client establishing mutual understanding coupled with collaborative efforts. There was a "client" only after there was clarification of the nature of the reciprocal roles and working relationships; for, in the end, the client was expected to become an active participant in a relationship with the worker. "Casework is a collaborative enterprise that can proceed successfully only when there is mutuality of understanding."[1]

FAMILY DIAGNOSIS: As the family constellation became an increasingly important factor in casework, the caseworker needed to acquire knowledge about an ever growing number of interacting forces. More recognition was given to the correlation between role functioning problems within the family and to the interaction between the neighborhood, the community, and the family. It was recognized that members of the family belong to more than one social system and that they needed to integrate many roles in order to avoid inconsistencies, conflicts and tensions. The local neighborhood and community were seen as social systems and it was implicit that people identified with these social systems either positively or negatively. Thus, casework with families stressed three factors—the individual, the family group, and the social milieu. When there were problems in family relationships, it was considered likely that there would be problems in other social relationships. In order to arrive at a family diagnosis, the caseworker had to determine which set of

[1] Pollack: *op. cit.,* p. 324.

influences most strongly molded attitudes and behavior traits, whether the influences were idiosyncratic, whether they were culturally patterned, and which had priority.

It was known that the client's presented problem was often used by him as a defense maneuver in order to avoid facing deeper-lying problems. Caseworkers endeavored to get to the real source of the difficulties and directed their efforts to understanding the interaction between the various family members. They then sought to reduce the points of undue conflict and strain. It was believed a definite improvement would be apparent when the focal sources of the difficulty were relieved. Since help was directed toward strengthening healthy ego defenses and adaptive patterns, caseworkers had to distinguish between healthy and pathological defenses. They, therefore, looked for such key items as motivation, verbal communication, and the role assigned to language and verbal exchange, as well as the capacity to use a professional helping relationship. As the client was able to initiate perceptual, cognitive and behavioral changes, the caseworker gave emotional support. Casework techniques of clarification, interpretation and confrontation were used but always with consideration being given to timing, client's readiness, and suitability of the content to be discussed.

During this era, an effort was made to study, objectively, how social and personal, that is inner and outer control measures could be used in the casework process.

> We know, psychodynamically, social approval is an important factor in the incorporation of values. Social approval includes the worker's approval, which can be a powerful dynamic when experienced by the client . . . Among other things, the caseworker must make clear that he stands for the rights of others, for lawful procedures, and solutions by reason and justice . . .[1]

In the past, use of control measures in casework had been largely frowned upon due to clients having been mistreated by family

---

[1] Irvin Weisman and Jacob Chwast, Ph.D.: Control and value in social work treatment, *Social Casework*, XLI, November, 1960, p. 456.

members or others outside the immediate family at points through-out his life span and with possible injurious effects.

COMMUNICATION: In working with families it was found that some were unable to communicate effectively. When such cases were discovered, the gradual re-establishment of communication was one of the most important aids in helping family members become "real persons" to each other.

In those families whose difficulties were rooted in interaction, the client was the "family group" and it was found that their significant conflicts and individual needs emerged more quickly and change was manifested earlier than in individual casework treatment. The trend in interviewing techniques was toward joint and family interviews. The home visit was emphasized, even to the worker's partaking of a meal or other hospitality in order to learn more about the family.

SOCIAL HISTORIES: Use of the social history, when indicated, has always helped the caseworker to understand the nature of the client's problems, to evaluate client strengths, to determine his ability to perform various social roles, and to understand more fully how he has been able to meet reality situations. Social histories often give a clearer picture of the interrelationships and are of assistance in evaluating the socio-economic situation and the cultural background of the client or family. However, during the early sixties more emphasis was being placed on the current social situation.

Treatment Goals

SOCIAL FUNCTIONING: Casework treatment involved evaluation of role commitments, role performance and culturally conditioned value orientations of family members. Casework with families had developed to three levels of service; first, family centered treatment with goals to affect development of social functioning of both individual and family members; second, enhancing roles of family members outside the family through group work and recreational service in the neighborhood. The neighborhood was seen as a medium that offered many opportunities for successful role functioning. The third level was intervention on a community-wide basis through use and coordination of multiple agencies and resources in order to help families understand and use community resources. This level of service could also be used to help agencies adjust their professional and administrative functioning to meet the current special needs of multi-problem families.[1] The general aim of casework treatment was to improve the social functioning of both the individual and the family unit of which the client was a member.

Treatment goals still needed to be more sharply delineated, case by case, with an emphasis on the clearer distinction between the current stress situation and the client's impaired functioning in his social role. Care also had to be taken not to overlook the immediate treatment goals for the long-term goals. With the continued efforts to integrate socio-dynamics and psycho-dynamics, the aim in treatment was to help clients function in their social roles as a way of more fully realizing their selfhood and their identity.

SUMMARY OF THE EARLY 1960'S

Social Change

The social changes in the early part of the sixties were occurring in a world of science and technology in which man tended to feel displaced. The period was referred to as the Age of the Anxious Sixties. The fate of the individual was seen to be closely related to the fate of the group. The trend of the times continued to place emphasis on more conformity as the individual must "fit" into the scheme of things.

The Family

The on-the-move American family was fast becoming still more "self-liquidating" resulting in a mobile society. Family members were encountering problems centered around lack of controls, with more acting out, more "guilt-free feelings," and a tendency

---

[1] Ludwig Geismar: Three levels of treatment for the multi-problem family, *Social Casework*, XLII, March, 1961, p. 127.

toward blaming others for adverse conditions or problems which were encountered.

The Caseworker

Caseworkers were clarifying their roles, and a tendency toward self-examination was evident. As the pendulum swung to the group process, caseworkers became more task-oriented; their role being to discover and to observe family interaction, to be aware of the impact of the environment on personality, and of the individual's adaptation in society and the family. In the early sixties, caseworkers placed renewed emphasis on the social functioning of individuals and on helping the family with problem solving.

The search for new dimensions in casework continued, a search for ways to relate psychological, somatic, social and cultural factors.

Casework

Further exploration was needed, particularly in relation to family diagnosis, to determine how the many roles of the individual in the family group and the social milieu could be integrated. The major casework goals of the early sixties were to improve the social functioning of the individual and the family as a unit.

REFERENCES

Articles

Cooper, Shirley: New trends in work with parents: progress or change? *Social Casework, XLII:* 7:342-347, July 1961.

Faucett, Emily: A re-evaluation of the home visit in casework practice, *Social Casework, XLII:* 9:439-445, November 1961.

Geismar, Ludwig: Three levels of treatment for the multi-problem family, *Social Casework, XLII:* 3:124-127, March 1961.

Geist, Joanne, and Gerber, Norman M.: Joint interviewing: a treatment technique with marital partners, *Social Casework, XLI:* 2: 76-83, February 1960.

Hellenbrand, Shirley C.: Client value orientations: implications for diagnosis and treatment, *Social Casework, XLII:* 4:163-169, April 1961.

Lazarus, Esther: The influence of the social structure on casework practice with the aging, *Social Casework*, *XLII:* 5-6, 227-233, May-June 1961.

Marcus, Mildred Rendl, Ph.D.: Women in the labor force, *Social Casework*, *XLI:* 6:298-302, June 1960.

McCormick, Mary J.: The role of values in social functioning, *Social Casework*, *XLII:* 2:70-78, February 1961.

McLain, Osborne: Social work in a public housing project, *Social Casework*, *XLI:* 8:408-418, October 1960.

Mitchell, Celia Brody: The use of family sessions in the diagnosis and treatment of disturbances in children, *Social Casework*, *XLI:* 6: 283-290, June 1960.

Montgomery, Dorothy S.: Relocation and its impact on families. *Social Casework*, *XLI:* 8:402-407, October 1960.

Perlman, Helen Harris: Intake and some role considerations, *Social Casework*, *XLI:* 4:171-177, April 1960.

Pollak, Otto and Brieland, Donald: The midwest seminar on family diagnosis and treatment, *Social Casework*, *XLII:* 7:319-324, July 1961.

Pollak, Otto, Young, Hazel M., and Leach, Helen: Differential diagnosis and treatment of character disturbances, *Social Casework*, *XLI:* 10:512-517, December 1960.

Regensburg, Jeanette: Implications for the practice of social casework, *Social Casework*, *XLI:* 1:13-18, January 1960.

Rostas, Ilona, D. So. Sc: Casework treatment of mothers in behalf of their children, *Social Casework*, *XLI:* 2:69-76, February 1960.

Siporin, Max: The concept of social types in casework theory and practice, *Social Casework*, *XLI:* 5:234-242, May 1960.

Stroup, Herbert: A historical explanation of alienation, *Social Casework*, *XLII:* 3:107-111, March 1961.

Teicher, Morton I: The culture of concepts, *Social Casework*, *XLII:* 10:491-493, December 1961.

Towle, Charlotte: Social work: cause and function, 1961, *Social Casework*, *XLII:* 8:385-397, October 1961.

Weisman, Irving, and Chwast, Jacob, Ph.D.: Control and value in social work treatment, *Social Casework*, *XLI:* 9:451-456, November 1960.

Chapter VII

CONCEPTUALIZATION,
PERIOD 1920 THROUGH 1961

> *Knowledge of truth alone does not suffice. On the contrary, this knowledge must continually be renewed by ceaseless effort, if it is not to be lost. It resembles a statue of marble which stands in the desert and is continuously threatened with burial by the shifting sand.*
>
> ALBERT EINSTEIN

SOCIAL CHANGE

The Search for Truth

IN THE PRECEDING chapters emphasis was on the practice of social casework, decade by decade. The purpose was to examine how social change affected the family and how casework progressed, decade by decade, to meet the needs of the family. The period of the early sixties, more than previous decades, is characterized by the fact that caseworkers are involved in assimilating an ever increasing body of new knowledge and acquiring a deeper understanding of the old.

The trend in casework is toward the use of socio-dynamics with emphasis on the social system and interpersonal relationships. Formerly the emphasis was on psycho-dynamics with use of psychiatric nomenclature. Based on knowledge of human growth and behavior, the casework focus was on the individual client and his psychological difficulties. During the early sixties there was evidence of a need to integrate the socio-dynamic and psycho-dynamic frame of reference. A lack of general casework principles and of systematized concepts was apparent and the rich virgin soil of concept potentialities remained unploughed.

Since theory development and experimental research are basic tools in the search for truth and development of new knowledge leading to optimum professional services, the actual dynamics of theory development needs to be specifically spelled out.

Theory Development

Theory is the knowledge of the principles and methods of an art or science rather than actual practice. Casework principles may be defined as truths, or even as doctrines; and these principles make up a philosophy, an accepted base. It is, however, of primary importance that such a set of basic principles or "beliefs" does not become static as changes may need to be made due to increased knowledge. From the basic principles flows a system of concepts, that are generalizations. For example, a few principles in casework on which there seems to be a high degree of agreement are: (1) the holistic principle: Personality is always an individual whole . . . ; (2) that both internal and environmental factors affect an individual's adjustment, and that (3) there is an interaction between internal and environmental forces.[1]

Thus, theory is made up of a philosophy (basic principles) that has applicable universal concepts, while casework practice is the unique application of the theory. In essence, theory is knowing and is based on the process of generalizing, while practice refers to doing and is characterized by specificity.

Four major reasons can be cited to support an increasing need for theory development: (a) the complexities and subtleties of social casework; (b) the need to move ahead with the times, particularly in view of the fact that social development is lagging behind technological development; (c) there exists a proliferation of divergent points of view among caseworkers, and (d) despite some indication of a rapprochement, there are conflicting schools of thought in the practice and theory of casework.

Social casework is still a "young" profession engaged in the process of growth and maturation and is especially dependent on the behavioral and more currently the social sciences. The current trend in the field of social work is to glean knowledge

---

[1] Callman Rawley: A sampling of expert opinion and some principles of casework, *Social Casework*, XXXV, April, 1954, p. 154.

from the social sciences of cultural anthropology, sociology and social psychology, economic and political science and to combine this knowledge to develop theories, concepts and ideas. There is a need for a closer partnership between the social sciences leading to a fusion of concepts and the reformulation of those concepts into new concepts—a bringing together of components to make a new whole. This involves the relating of cultural, social, somatic and psychological factors. Fortunately, the gap between the different disciplines appears to be narrowing. Each discipline, however, is still a well defined group, renders an apparently specialized service to the community, has its own special methods and terminology, and "thinks as a group." Gordon Hamilton referred to the hard task of each profession's defining its goals and making education and training adequate for its *shared* responsibility.[1] All of the disciplines feel the lack of knowledge in their own fields. This lag in theory development in all disciplines only puts more onus on social caseworkers to continue theory development in relation to the growing body of experience.

> Growth can be frightening, but the western world in which these professions are reared has come to look upon sound growth as something good leading to something better . . . that a new profession can attain this position (understanding of their responsibility) after a half century of growth promises well for its developing powers and future progress.[2]

The practitioner gleans knowledge from the scientist, and the scientist learns from the practitioner. What is needed is the clear awareness and perspective of the multiplicity of factors involved in this process. Theory development must be based on appropriate methods and must have clearly defined objectives. In addition, theory development should employ the tools of well defined terminology and tested methods to attain more thorough

---

[1] Gordon Hamilton: The role of social casework in social policy, *Social Casework*, XXXIII, October, 1952, p. 323.

[2] Jean M. Snelling: 'Professional leadership in the social structure, *Social Casework*, XXXV, July, 1954, p. 279.

knowledge and to contribute significantly to the growth of theory formation in the field of social casework. There is an urgent need to press a search for greater oneness in spite of diversity, for in spite of diversity there are common problems. For example: Both the reality, and the individuality of clients' problems are obscured by the lack of well-defined psycho-dynamic and related socio-dynamic concepts. Identifying a *unifying concept* is a step on the way to developing a theory.

Concepts

A concept can be referred to as a general or generalized notion of a highly schematized idea. A concept should represent the real essence of the objects included under it. It can be a process which means or refers to one object in relation to others. Finally, a concept is an abstract idea. Concepts enable us to generalize. Put in another way, a concept is general, it is an abstract generalization; it is the abstraction and generalization from sense impressions or ideas. A concept is a universal perception; it cannot be specific, in the sense of being unique; it must be an abstract generalization. Abstract entities are essentially "unbound" and therefore are of necessity universal.

A KEY CONCEPT is the "actual genesis," the core. In 1920, Ada Sheffield was one of the first to refer to key concepts. Determining what is significant, interpreting facts, means relating to key concepts. These key concepts form a constellation of concepts. In other words, as a rule no single factor explains a situation or difficulty. A social summary may give many factors. *A key concept is a "larger" idea that may have sub-factors bearing a relationship or may further define the concept:* For example, "bad housing"—unsanitary living conditions, or "child neglect"—children alone at night, children not properly fed. To use an analogy —"In poetry, the significance of the key line, around which other mental images began to cluster like needles around a lodestone."[1]

Gordon Hamilton, in referring to the profession of casework, emphasized the need for intellectual means of communicating and

---

1 Marginal Notes: *The Family,* February, 1921, p. 15.

reviewing experience, for "fundamental differences at the periphery, accepted and respected, make for growth; fundamental differences at the *core* make for schisms or nullification, retard the mobility of workers, lead to all sorts of crippling misunderstandings."[1] Specifically referring to the concept of self-determination, Helen Perlman stated, "We need to pierce the shell of certain concepts that have become shibboleths among us, to seek for the core of their actual meaning and to try to establish their particular relationship to social casework practice."[2]

GENERIC CONCEPTS: We are all part of a common society. Most have been raised in families that share broad basic similarities. There is an underlying unity in human nature, and in our experiences, that makes it possible for us to understand each other. We can identify a recurrent theme in human behavior, as well as the differences. There is a richness of knowledge and understanding that can be used when the common factors are recognized, the knowledge that other human beings travel the same road and have common needs.

> The wider our knowledge of 'likeness' in behavior the more fully shall we comprehend the meaning of the feelings and action of people with whom we are working . . . Both individualization and generalization are needed."[3]

The "relationship" is a generic concept that has its parts—acceptance, non-judgmental attitude, individualization, client self-determination.

OPERATIONAL CONCEPTS: There is a gap between actual practice and theory. A concept is universal; using the concept, or the concept in operation, is being specific; it is applying the theory. Concepts flow from the principles that make up the philosophy of casework.

---

[1] Gordon Hamilton: The underlying philosophy of social casework, *The Family*, XXII, July, 1941, p. 139.

[2] Helen Harris Perlman: The casework use of collateral information, *Social Casework*, XXXII, October, 1951, p. 325.

[3] Florence Hollis: The relationship between psychosocial diagnosis and treatment, *Social Casework*, XXXII, February, 1951, p. 67.

How *is* the generic related to the specific? It was the belief of some writers that one way to shorten the gap between practice and theory was to make concepts "more whole" and to define them operationally. They also believed that basic principles and certain conditions needed to be spelled out in order to have workable concepts. Many caseworkers would have operational concepts to explain the purpose of concepts and describe how they are used in practice. They felt this was necessary because, if basic concepts were capable of various interpretations, two people could agree on them and still be "miles apart" in their understanding of the concept and the way it is used in practice. Some caseworkers felt that if concepts were defined operationally as they apply in unique situations that this would bridge the gap between theory (universal concepts) and practice (the unique application). Some concepts are vague as a result of the caseworker's own limited or obscure thinking, while some concepts remain vague because their component factors have not been clearly identified by scientific research. This means that some concepts will be more clearly defined or revised through time. Caseworkers can make a significant contribution to the body of knowledge by identifying component parts of a concept. Their observations need to go into recordings.

One of the fundamental questions which has been raised from the early beginnings of the profession was "How is a concept used in practice?" It was the belief of some writers that a good grasp of well defined and clearly relevant concepts which were both concrete and applicable would help the caseworker more quickly gain self-reliance.

In reality, however, there is only one way to bridge the gap between theory and practice and that is through experience. As caseworkers become imbued with concepts and casework principles, the concepts become increasingly internalized and a fusion between conceptual knowledge and experiential knowledge grows and deepens. "It is what you do with what you have . . . in the way of a concept that really tests how you understand the concept and how effective it is in your practice."[1] *This fusion or*

---

1 Rawley: *op. cit.*, page 157.

bridging the gap between theory and practice can only be experienced and lived.

Conceptualization

There are a few caseworkers who question the process of conceptualization. They wonder whether conceptual generalizations are possible or desirable due to the complexity of casework. They consider casework to be one of the subtlest and most elusive of all techniques as "it addresses itself to social relationships, intangible, invisible and imponderable."[1]

Other caseworkers believe casework terminology, research questions, concepts and principles are vague, inarticulate, unknown and inadequately defined. Even though many caseworkers accept the proposition that clearer concepts are needed, little progress has been made toward correcting the problem. Of approximately one thousand articles in twenty volumes of *"Social Casework,"* only twenty-seven articles were noted to have a measure of concern about the details of some aspect of conceptualization.[2]

Experimental Research

Experimental research is another method of developing casework theory. A major purpose of research is to discover likenesses and to find unifying concepts. A fundamental of the scientific method is problem solution. The substance of developing new knowledge includes uncovering unperceived gaps in previous knowledge. Reference has been made to the lack of accepted diagnostic categories, the lack of definite formulation of concepts and to the fact that there is some disagreement on basic concepts. Some writers have expressed the opinion that the two schools of thought, the Functional and the Diagnostic, reflected a lack of unity in the profession and limited the ability for casework to

---

[1] Gordon Hamilton: Refocusing family casework, *The Family,* XII, October, 1931, p. 175.

[2] Helen Brenenstul: *The Development of Social Casework Theory,* Unpublished Thesis, School of Social Welfare, University of Ottawa, Ottawa, Canada, 1958.

proceed with some of the further steps required for professional growth. Others felt different schools of thought are bound to arise, that the problem was really how to blend and integrate the two schools but that this presented difficulties. As Gordon Hamilton wrote: ". . . we could not easily resolve the problem [of the two schools of thought] unless we have objectively minded persons starting from unlike disciplines studying and reporting on the same cases."[1]

The goals and aims of experimental research in casework are often focused on evaluating casework theory, including basic casework assumptions and principles, uncovering the rationale of current techniques, discovery of more effective techniques, evaluating treatment, discovering new concepts of psycho- and socio-dynamics.

The explicit areas in research that need more emphasis are: (a) knowledge about the methodology and content of casework; (b) the rationale of casework techniques; (c) methods or means of evaluating casework; (d) knowledge about psychodynamics of the individual; (e) knowledge about the human emotions, and socio-dynamics such as interpersonal relationships; (f) chronic cases, and (g) finally, increased knowledge about families, "what makes families right?", "what is a strong family?", "assessment of family strengths," "the dynamics of family life."

Research may use conceptualization methods such as application of formal logic, or a combination of both reasoning and data collection accomplished by "the descriptive stage . . . relevant facts are observed and conceptualized in the form of systems of classification; and the inductive-deductive stage, in which the relationship between facts is observed and conceptualized in the form of general laws with predictive power."[2]

Problems involved in carrying out experimental research are economic, social, psychological and methodological. "The economic problem" is the high cost of research, thus making it diffi-

---

1 Hamilton: The underlying philosophy of social casework, p. 143.

2 Hilde Landenberger Hochwald: The function of social work research, *Social Casework*, XXXIV, January, 1953, p. 29.

cult to raise funds. Also the community at large may not be "sold" on research.

The social problems involved in research relate to community prejudices. There are still those who subscribe to a sort of pseudo-Darwinism believing that a person failing in the struggle to survive is inferior and an intrinsically puritanic tradition—"the poor are poor because of their sins and whatever they get is good for them."[1]

Psychological problems arise in relation to caseworkers who have deep resistances to research due to a conflict in methods of looking at the nature of man . . . "yet it is surely true that within the profession there is uneasiness and perhaps rejection among some workers who were not able to come to terms personally with psychology . . ." [and who feel the casework] . . . process is unrelated to human feelings and human existence.[2] Gordon Hamilton pointed out that caseworkers must "bring what they know of human behavior and interpersonal adaptations into the fabric of welfare and community life . . . as it will further knowledge in the field of social as well as psycho-dynamics." She further stated that there are social scientists who resist taking into account the conscious and unconscious feelings and motivation of man, and that these scientists need a broader knowledge of human behavior and interpersonal adaptations as they relate to human welfare, to the nature of man, and his relationship to his universe . . . that man needs to be able and willing to understand human personality.[3]

The methodological problems that appear are in relation to the subtleties and intricacies of social phenomena which seem to elude research because standard research tools are ill adapted to these complexities. There is the difficulty of devising statistical methods suitable to qualitative data as the elusive entities of the data, the intangibles, need to be broken down into their elements, to be "caught" and manipulated for research.

---

[1] Margaret Blenkner: Obstacles to evaluative research in casework: Part I, *Social Casework*, XXXI, February, 1950, p. 54.

[2] Snelling: *op. cit.*, p. 284.

[3] Hamilton: The role of social casework in social policy, p. 315.

Since the caseworkers' knowledge of research methods is largely limited, a need exists for more emphasis on training in research during the sequence of professional education. A need exists to develop new methods of research. Currently, new methods of research have appeared and are in the process of appearing. New techniques for utilizing computing devices, new uses of microfilm, photographic process, and new ways of recording have been added as aids in research. On the basis of progress to date, there is every reason to believe that the development of more exact research tools will make rapid progress.

As pointed out, the two generally accepted methods of developing casework theory are: (1) conceptualization, and (2) experimental research. There are, however, two additional supplemental steps: (1) the process of integrating the new knowledge as it develops, and (2) conveying the new knowledge to members of the casework profession. As new knowledge emerges, ideas develop in the course of time through thesis, antithesis, and integration. As these ideas are analyzed and synthesized, it is of great importance to make careful judgments as to their significance. It must also be remembered that the emphasis on knowledge can change as new perspectives develop. *There is a pressing need to amplify and spell out the processes of theory development in professional social casework if new knowledge based on research in casework practice is to be made available to members of the casework profession.*

THE CASEWORKER

Search for Knowledge

There is a tremendous spread of substantive knowledge caseworkers are now required to assimilate including such concepts as personality, behavior, interpersonal relationships and culture. Current scientific, economic, and political influences tend to indicate a trend to an ever increasing body of experience for all individuals. The continued efforts toward integration of both human growth and development theory and social theory during this current period have made it necessary for caseworkers to become equally familiar with socio-dynamics as with psycho-dynamics.

Clarification of Existing Concepts

A survey of casework literature revealed that most caseworkers felt there were specific areas of casework theory that needed more explicit conceptualization. They referred particularly to international concepts; educational concepts; the concept of authority in casework; the concept of the relationship; and the criteria for measuring success or failure in casework.

In regard to international concepts, one writer stated:

> " . . . as we exchange ideas about our national experience, we seem more inclined to think in terms of programs and organizational patterns rather than in terms of concepts and principles . . . that likenesses or differences in *services* catch the eye [rather than] differences in concepts about human problems and social phenomena."[1]

A few basic concepts on which there seemed to be some agreement were: (1) the individual has capacity to develop and change; (2) the feeling of being accepted . . . ; (3) positive experiences are growth promoting; (4) the family provides the main source of emotional support and satisfaction; (5) individuals have certain rights and privileges, and (6) forces affecting individual well-being are multiple and interacting.[2]

Kurt Freudenthal, commenting on concepts for education, wrote:

> The mode of communication of professional content for the purposes of teaching and interpretation remains fragmentary and therefore largely ineffective . . . It is the absence of systematized structured concepts by which we can effectively transmit to others knowledge about our principles and tech-

---

[1] Cora Kasius: Are social work principles emerging internationally, *Social Casework,* XXXIV, January, 1953, p. 24.

[2] *Ibid.*

niques which has made interpretation of social casework difficult . . . within our own ranks.[1]

Social work schools, through their educational methods for
casework, have gone to some lengths to help students grow emotionally. In contrast, the process of conceptualization is taught
indirectly, thus creating a sense of mystery and obscurity about
the methods of conceptualization. Eleanor Cockerill wrote:

> Training for professional adjustment [needed to be] to a world
> of emerging ideas rather than to a world of fixed doctrines . . .
> [that a student] needed to relinquish some of the very con-
> cepts in which he is being trained and to embrace new ideas
> as they emerge . . . [and that] a revolution in the organization
> of teaching content, media, method and man-power is already
> upon us . . .[2]

One author questioned the use of concepts in education stating
that students were caught in a dilemma in their knowing (intellectual) and feeling (emotional) learning experience. "Facts are
important and concepts are significant, but the essence of human
relationships is far too complex to be bounded by a fact, or concept, regardless of how elaborate or all-encompassing it may be."[3]

A number of caseworkers felt further conceptualization was
needed concerning authority and the use of authority in casework, social authority factors, and authority in the caseworker-
client relationship. Referring to the concept of the "relationship,"
some caseworkers believed it was important to be able to explain,
define and analyze the casework relationship, as a whole and in
its parts. "Even though a verbal explanation cannot adequately
convey the full human overtones in a good casework relationship
—the profession needs a good conceptual analysis of the casework

---

[1] Kurt Freudenthal: The why and how of casework research, *Social Casework*, XXXV,
July, 1954, p. 298.

[2] Eleanor Cockerill: The interdependence of the professions in helping people, *Social
Casework*, XXXIV, November, 1953, p. 377.

[3] Morton I. Teicher: The culture of concepts, *Social Casework*, XLII, December, 1961,
p. 492.

'relationship.' "[1] A few writers expressed disbelief that appropriate and useful abstract concepts of "relationship" could be formulated. They felt that the basis of the casework "relationship" was primarily an emotional one and that pure reason and the scientific spirit would not help.

Conceptualization is needed to establish more adequate criteria for measuring *success* and *failure* in casework:

> A multi-dimensional system for classifying diagnostically the families or individuals (the problem; the interpersonal situation; the psycho-dynamics) and a descriptive classification of the kinds of help given and a way to measure the skill with which help is given.[2]

The question was raised whether the degree of improvement *could* be equated with the degree of success as movement judgment say nothing about the *kind* of change that occurs *in* clients or, indeed, whether the change may not be in the client's *situations*.[3] There appeared to be a lack of criteria for knowing "what makes families right."

The fact that caseworkers wanted clarification of existing concepts would indicate that they were experiencing difficulty in the process of conceptualization itself. Some caseworkers felt they needed to study and learn to use the abstract process of conceptualization before they began to conceptualize, because they had not had an opportunity to study this process before. They wanted to learn the essentials of what conceptualization involved, how it blended with casework and the total process of "applying logic to casework."

Caseworker and Conceptualization

This lack of clarification of concepts and terminology could be due to the caseworkers' traditional ways of thinking. Due to

---

[1] Felix P. Biestek: An analysis of the casework relationship, *Social Casework*, XXXV, February, 1956, p. 57.

[2] McVidder J. Hunt, Leonard S. Kogan and Margaret Blenkner: A field test of the movement scale, *Social Casework*, XXXI, July, 1950, p. 274.

[3] *Ibid.*

heavy loads, and because social change creates further stress, some caseworkers have difficulty in changing their way of thinking. Others appeared to be resistive to the additional burden of "spotting likenesses" or "forms of relatedness" and engaging in the extensive and arduous labor which conceptualization requires.

The development of casework theory appears to be weakened by the lack of *individual* concern for invention and creative conceptual curiosity. Some caseworkers seem suspicious of searching for likenesses in behavior, motives and relationships. Also, the rapid increase in migration among caseworkers does not leave them free to do extensive thinking about general trends or the deeper issues of casework theory. The enormous spread of uncoordinated knowledge in need of assimilation, intensified by the complexity, variations and intangible aspect of the human personality, appears to present an overwhelming task.

Generalization vs. Specific

The caseworker's interest in powers of individualization seems to far exceed their interest in powers of generalization. Caseworkers appear to be more interested in personality and problem *differences* than in likenesses. "Our physical and mental endowments are more similar than dissimilar. We are part of a common society . . . We are by no means *identical* in our endowments and life experiences, but without question, we have much in common."[1] Caseworkers have skill in individualizing problems, but there appears to be a lack of interest or the ability to generalize. Their powers of verbalizing appear to be greater than the powers of coordinating ideas. This lack of generalization causes excessive individualization and fragmentation. They lean more toward the specific and seem to prefer to deal exclusively with concrete tools, techniques and skills, rather than to conceptualize.

Some caseworkers felt they were struggling with the problem of "not understanding each other" because of the lack of standardized definitions and because the "inner definitions" for central

---

[1] Hollis: *loc. cit.*

terms were different. The problem of "not understanding" might be related to a relative lack of controversy among caseworkers. Controversy is based on the assumption that by "daring to disagree" and through controversy and extensive dialogue and debate, a profession can come closer together in an understanding of issues, concepts and terms. This failure to disagree with colleagues may be related to

> . . . a misapplication of casework principles, [that is] because one does not argue with clients, one does not argue with professional colleagues; [that is] failure to distinguish between aggression and self-assertion and between social and unsocial competition, and personal and professional insecurity, making differences acceptable only in clients.[1]

Some caseworkers questioned the value of generalizations and asked if generalizations could truly represent the infinite variations of people functioning in a vast range of specific situations.

Resistances

Other caseworkers appeared to have strong resistances to conceptualization. These resistances seem to be traceable to deeply held beliefs that appropriate and useful abstract concepts can not be formulated in casework. This viewpoint was referred to as the intuitive as opposed to the logical school. Margaret Blenkner stated, "These biases the 'intuitive' and the 'logical' against each other operate inter-professionally as well as intra-professionally."[2] The intuitive school was concerned lest a "rigid science supercede a soul-satisfying art." They wanted "operational" concepts in an effort to determine the function of concepts. This intuitive point of view, it was felt, might be based on insecurity and the fact that they might not be achieving as much as they hoped to achieve. Also, some of the "intuitive" group believed experimental research would cause deterioration in casework because research would lead to "hard and fast rules."

---

[1] Roger W. Little: The literature of social casework, *Social Casework*, XXXIII, July, 1952, p. 287.

[2] Blenkner: *op. cit.*, p. 56.

A few caseworkers opposed all forms of "theory making" for fear of establishing "operational concepts." They felt casework was "emotional" and that pure reason, by way of generalization, would corrupt casework practice. Many caseworkers believed that if conceptualization had to be done, it should be carried out by committees and on a large scale and by schools of social work rather than by the caseworkers themselves. But as one writer put it, the prevalent "recurrent theme is always the same—caseworkers need such research, they must do it themselves, they are just on the verge of doing it, but they have not quite managed to get around to it."[1]

It would appear that an outstanding difficulty is represented by the attitudes of caseworkers toward conceptualization. Many have misconceptions, and conflicts about conceptualization coupled with some confusion about the relationship of "generalization" to the "unique." It must be recognized that if creative art in casework is to develop to a high degree, caseworkers need to develop the ability to conceptualize in order to function more knowingly and effectively. One of man's major means of discovery is to find likenesses between things. This means applying logic to casework—which involves both relating one and the many and sharing this knowledge through adequate communication.

CONCEPTUALIZATION

General Methods

DEFINITION: The process by which concepts are formulated is conceptualization. This is done by abstracting and generalizing from *sense* impressions and/or *ideas;* that is, *conceptualization is forming the abstract significance of sense impressions or ideas.* In conceptualization, the relationship of the specific to the generic is the same dynamic and intensely close interaction that exists between mind and body, the non-material and material, the abstract and concrete. The concrete comes before the abstract, the deed before the word. The path to be travelled is going from

---

[1] *Ibid.*

the concrete (the "facts"), the starting point, to the goal, the abstract.

Procedure and Techniques

SPOTTING LIKENESSES: The procedure is to recognize and abstract the significance of sense impressions. This process of spotting likenessess requires extensive, arduous labor. The abstract methods of achieving this could be: (1) by gathering of ideas, analysis and synthesis; (2) through different types of definition such as—a) Aristotelian, which involves genus and species, and b) descriptive, and (3) by the process of formal logic, which might be—a) *deductive:* a deductive syllogism involving two premises with a conclusion from the two premises—from a generalization to the particular, or b) *inductive:* from the particular to generalization . . . "from a part to a whole . . . a creative reasoning mode by means of which the store of man's knowledge may be gradually increased;" and c) *diagnostic reasoning mode:* by proceeding from the particular and a generalization, as premises to a diagnostic conclusion.[1]

A number of even more concrete and practical means of conceptualization would be:

a) Through use of the cumulative literature, each contributor systematically building on earlier material, and systematizing his observations. This is accomplished by:
   a) thesis, b) antithesis and c) synthesis;
b) By studies of the literature;
c) By analysis of concepts in other disciplines such as social and natural sciences and creative arts;
d) Through more generalizations in day-to-day records;
e) By defining terminology to establish more general agreement throughout the field;
f) By defining research questions and conceptual criteria for experimental research, and;

---

[1] Louis J. Lehrman: The logic of diagnosis, *Social Casework,* XXXV, May, 1954, p. 192.

g) By additional conceptualizing of current concepts, principles and theory;

h) By developing new concepts.

Aims and Goals

SEARCH FOR TRUTH: The specific aims to be achieved in conceptualization would be to formulate more generic, operational and key concepts. There is a need for more precise definitions, more explicit terminology and new dimensions in understanding and insight. Fundamental conceptual differences in points of view, values and ideologies should be explored. Clear and well defined research questions must be developed. Last, but not least, additional objectives such as new insights need to be put into words, to be translated into crystallized concepts and made available to new caseworkers entering the field. Those already in the field need to keep abreast of new content, and current changes—particularly as new discoveries change the meaning of old concepts.

In general, "It is a well-founded historical generalization that the last thing to be discovered in any science is what the science is really about. Men go on groping for centuries, guided merely by a dim instinct and a puzzled curiosity, till at last 'some great truth is loosened.' "[1]

> The only way in which human institutions develop seems to be by too much emphasis at a time on one aspect of the truth, with neglect, during the period, of the compensating opposites. In later stages of growth, the emphasis is shifted to different aspects of truth, until in time a vision of Truth in its full beauty will dawn on us.[2]

It is clearly evident that the profession has established a sound core of accumulated knowledge and that the growing outer edge of principally new knowledge is being extended rapidly. This leaves the profession with the challenge of our times—to find new

---

[1] M. Antoinette Cannon: Recent changes in the philosophy of social workers, *The Family*, XIV, October, 1933, p. 193.

[2] Lyra Taylor: Emotion and Social Casework, *The Family*, XII, January, 1952, p. 272.

ways to assure rapid communication and application of new knowledge and, at the same time, to foster optimum growth of the expanding outer periphery of knowledge.

SUMMARY

Social Change

Rapid social change brings about a growing body of experience and an ever increasing content of knowledge. This, in turn, creates a need to bridge the gap between practice and theory in casework. Theory development is based on the process of generalization and is the search for knowledge and new dimensions. Casework principles make up a philosophy and an accepted base. From these basic principles flow a system of concepts. Thus, theory development means knowing, leading to concept formation. Two methods of theory development are distinguished: (1) by conceptualization, and (2) through experimental research. A final and necessary step is the integrating of this new knowledge as it develops and conveying it to the members of the casework profession.

The Caseworker

The trend to an ever increasing range of professional experience means caseworkers must assimilate a spread of substantive knowledge in the areas of personality, human behavior, interpersonal relationships, culture, economic and political influences. The task of assimilating this largely uncoordinated body of knowledge seems overwhelming. There is evidence that caseworkers lean more toward being specific rather than to the process of generalization and that they need to do more conceptualizing. The caseworker's traditional ways of thinking may be based on their misconceptions and conflicts in regard to the relationship of generalization to the unique.

Conceptualization

The general method of conceptualization consists of formulating abstract significance from sense impressions or ideas. The tools of discovery are spotting likenesses between things and recognizing as well as abstracting the significance of sense impressions. A number of aims and goals of conceptualization are recognized: (1) more generic, key and operational concepts; (2) more precise definitions, and (3) more explicit terminology. A need exists to find more effective ways of exploring and communicating experience in order to achieve new dimensions in understanding and insight and to put these into words which are meaningful to members of the social work profession.

THE OUTLOOK AND THE PROMISE

All evidence points to the fact that social work, as a profession stands on the threshold of a major growth era. The quality of the articles of professional writers, the proliferation of significant published research and the fresh and vital currents of controversy and open-ended dialogue, plus a renewed interest in "social action," all give promise that the profession is entering a new plane of growth. It is hoped that by tracing the development of social casework vis-a-vis social change and change in the family, yeast will be added to this ferment.

If we can gain a clearer understanding of the main stems and roots of casework theory and practice as it exists today, we are in a favored position to discern where further growth and development is needed. Similar to the good gardener who knows when his plants need nutrients and care, a profession can have the discernment and self-awareness to bend its efforts to foster growth and development in selected areas. The degree to which such energy and effort is channeled into these nodal areas of growth is an index to the maturity of the profession.

Perhaps the most promising areas which can have an immediate and far ranging impact on the profession are areas of theory development and concept formation and the area of social work research. As the energies of members of the profession are directed into these areas in a thoughtful and planned way, and as the profession assumes responsibility for leadership and coordination in such an effort, *this can lead not only to a vast improvement in services to the clients, but it can place social work in a position to make a major contribution to the related "helping professions."* It is hoped that this study will stimulate intra- and inter-professional dialogue resulting in conscious and planned professional growth.

REFERENCES

Unpublished Material

Brenenstul, Helen: "The Development of Social Casework Theory." Unpublished Masters Thesis, Graduate School of Social Welfare, University of Ottawa, Ottawa, Canada, 1958.

Otto, Herbert: "The Otto Family Strength Survey." Graduate School of Social Work, University of Utah, Salt Lake City, Utah.

Articles

Berl, Fred: An Attempt to Construct a Conceptual Framework for Supervision, *Social Casework, XLI:* 7: 339-346, July, 1960.

Biestek, Felix P. S. J.: An Analysis of the Casework Relationship. *Social Casework, XXXV:* 2: 57-61, February, 1954.

Blenkner, Margaret: Obstacles to Evaluative Research in Casework: Part I. *Social Casework, XXXI:* 2: 54-60, February, 1950.

Cannon, M. Antoinette: Recent Changes in the Philosophy of Social Workers, *The Family, XIV:* 6: 193-198, October, 1933.

Cockerill, Eleanor: The Interdependence of the Professions in Helping People. *Social Casework, XXXIV:* 9: 371-378, November, 1953.

Freudenthal, Kurt: The Why and How of Casework Research. *Social Casework, XXXV:* 7: 296-298, July, 1954.

Hamilton, Gordon: Refocusing Family Casework. *The Family, XII:* 6: 174-183, October, 1931.

————: The Role of Social Casework in Social Policy. *Social Casework, XXXIII:* 8: 315-324, October, 1952.

————: The Underlying Philosophy of Social Casework. *The Family, XXII:* 5: 139-147, July, 1941.

Hochwald, Hilde Landenberger: The Function of Social Work Research. *Social Casework, XXXIV:* 1: 29-33, January, 1953.

Hollis, Florence: The Relationship Between Psychosocial Diagnosis and Treatment. *Social Casework, XXXII:* 2: 67-74, February, 1951.

Hunt, McVidder J., Kogan, Leonard S. and Blenkner, Margaret: A Fieldtest of the Movement Scale. *Social Casework, XXXI:* 7: 267-277, July, 1950.

Kasius, Cora: Are Social Work Principles Emerging Internationally? *Social Casework, XXXIV:* 1: 23-29, January, 1953.

Lehrman, Louis J.: The Logic of Diagnosis. *Social Casework, XXXV:* 5: 192-199, May, 1954.

Little, Roger W.: The Literature of Social Casework. *Social Casework, XXXIII:* 7: 287-291, July, 1952.

Marginal Notes: *The Family. I:* 1: 15, February, 1921.

Perlman, Helen Harris: The Caseworker's Use of Collateral Information. *Social Casework. XXXII:* 8: 325-333, October, 1951.

Rawley, Callman: A Sampling of Expert Opinion on Some Principles of Casework. *Social Casework, XXXV:* 4: 154-161, April, 1954.

Snelling, Jean M.: Professional Leadership in the Social Structure. *Social Casework, XXXV:* 7: 279-284, July, 1954.

Taylor, Lyra: Emotion and Social Casework, *The Family, XII:* 9: 272-274, January, 1932.

Teicher, Morton I.: The Culture of Concepts. *Social Casework, XLII:* 10: 491-493, December, 1961.

AUTHOR INDEX .

SUBJECT INDEX

A

Abstracting, 164-165
Acceptance, 118-119
Adaptive patterns, modified, 121
Adolescents', problems of, 108
Aged, 109-110, 133
Agencies, private, 7-9
  authority, 114
  casework services, 25-26
  client's fear of, 110
  closed doors, 56
  community planning, 113
  fee charging, 82, 114
  open door, 112
  private practice, 114-115, 123
  relief giving, 26, 55-57, 71
  social action, 113
Aggressive casework, 109
Agricultural economy, 18-19
Alienation, man's, 130
Almshouse, 5, 8-9
Anxious sixties, age of, 146
Aristotelian logic, 165. *Also see* Conceptualization, techniques
Artistic skill, casework, 163
Assistance, financial. *See* Money
Authority, caseworker, 114, 135
Authority, concept, 160
Authority, family, 58, 79
Automation, age of, 102, 122-123, 131-132

B

Behavior patterns, changing, 133
Behavioral theory. *See* Human growth and behavior
Bureaucracies, 104, 122

C

Case records, 26, 96-97
  chronological recording, 27-28
  fact finding, 27-31
  group work recording, 135
  recording interviews, an outline, 44-47
  topical recording, 27-28
Case study method, research, 29-31, 61-62
Casework, 17-18, 36-42, 63-70, 85-97, 116-122, 142, 146. *Also see* Casework, general methods; Casework techniques; Casework, treatment goals
  achievement, 31
  aggressive, 109
  artistic skill, 35, 163
  definitions, 14-15, 33-35, 139
  generic, 61
  problem entities, need for, 141
  scientific process, 35, 163
  social diagnosis defined, 17
  social diagnosis, fluid, 97
  specialization, 15, 61
  therapy, as, 61, 64, 70
Casework, family centered. *See* Family centered casework
Casework, general methods, 17, 36-38, 63-65, 85-89, 116, 142
  diagnostic school, 86-88. *Also see* Diagnostic school
  differential diagnosis, 64, 66, 71
  direct and indirect, 64
  external and internal factors, 63-64, 116
  functional school, 85-86, 98. *Also see* Functional school
  group method, 135, 142
  indirect and direct, 64
  internal and external factors, 63-64, 116
  needs, identifying, 63
  new dimensions, 142

173

Date Due